The Pope and Revolution

The Pope and Revolution

John Paul II Confronts Liberation Theology

John Paul II   Gustavo Gutiérrez
Michael Novak   James V. Schall, S.J.
Dale Vree

Edited by Quentin L. Quade
Foreword by Richard John Neuhaus

Ethics and Public Policy Center
Washington, D.C.

#8346790

Library of Congress Cataloging in Publication Data
Main entry under title:
The Pope and revolution.
   Bibliography: p.
   Includes index.
   1. Liberation theology—Addresses, essays, lectures.
2. Christianity and politics—Addresses, essays, lectures.
3. Conferencia General del Episcopado Latinoamericano
(3rd : 1979 : Puebla, Mexico)—Addresses, essays, lectures.
4. John Paul II, Pope, 1920-   —Addresses, essays,
lectures.   5. Catholic Church—Latin America—Addresses,
essays, lectures.   I. Gutiérrez, Gustavo, 1928-
BT83.57.P64   261.7   82-4971
ISBN 0-89633-059-1   AACR2
ISBN 0-89633-054-0 pbk.

$11.50 cloth, $7.00 paper

94035

Contents

APPENDIXES

From the Medellín Statement,
Latin American Bishops, 1968:

From the Puebla Statement,
Latin American Bishops, 1979:

Foreword

By Richard John Neuhaus

THE QUESTIONS ENGAGED BY this volume are of ecumenical importance, because all the churches—mainline Protestant, Orthodox, Lutheran, and evangelical, as well as Roman Catholic—are embroiled in thinking through the nature of Christian responsibility for the social and political order. The questions are also of ecumenical importance because non-Catholic Christians increasingly recognize that any advance toward Christian unity requires the full participation and even the leadership of the Roman Catholic Church. Because it is the largest Christian communion and because it has the potential of providing an institutional centering for a more unified Christianity, the directions taken by Roman Catholicism must be of urgent concern to all who share the ecumenical vision.

A third reason why the questions addressed in this volume are of ecumenical importance is that the *oikoumene,* the household of God, is intended to encompass the whole of humankind. How the Christian community relates to the politics of the modern world is not simply an in-house question of interest to the several churches or to all of them together. If, as Christians claim, the Gospel of the coming Kingdom of God is the promised future of humankind, then how that Gospel is related to the "principalities and powers" of the present time is a matter of world-historical importance.

The perennial temptation of Christians over the centuries has been to settle for something less than the Kingdom of God. We can do this either by accommodating to the way things are, or by confusing the Kingdom of God with our programs for making things the way we think they ought to be. Thus settling for something less than the Kingdom can assume either "conservative" or "radical" forms. In the fourth century the Christian historian Eusebius saw the Kingdom of God in the union of church and empire under Constantine. Somewhat later, with the Roman Empire falling around him, a disillusioned Augustine magisterially distinguished between the City of God and the City of Man. The Constantinian accommodation would rise again in appearances as diverse as the Holy Roman Empire of Charlemagne, Calvin's grandly flawed experiment in Geneva, and Puritan New England's "city upon a hill." In the last century and into the early part of this one, the Kingdom of God was frequently identified with the extension of Western Christian civilization. Today, almost as a mirror image of earlier illusions, it is often posited that demolishing the social, economic, and political orders of that same civilization is necessary to establish the Kingdom of God.

Among Protestant and Orthodox Christians, the World Council of Churches is the chief bearer of the ecumenical vision. A traditional theme of the WCC has been "The Unity of the Church— The Unity of Humankind," meaning that unity among Christians is a sign and instrument of the unity of humankind. In the workings and pronouncements of the WCC today it sometimes seems that the logic has been reversed, and that the unity of humankind—to be achieved by social and political changes called "liberation"— will define the unity of the Church. Various liberation theologies speak of "the partisan Church" that is composed of all those who engage in the struggle for "systemic" change of societal structures.

Among Protestants as among Roman Catholics, those who adopt this liberationist view acknowledge their indebtedness to "Marxist analysis." Many go farther and describe themselves as Christian Marxists, and, in specific situations of conflict, almost all declare their sympathies to be with the forces self-professed as Marxist-Leninist. Such sympathy, they say, is not impelled merely by prudential judgment but is a matter of cooperating with what God is doing in history. God is working liberation, and liberation is what the Bible means by salvation. What Eusebius saw in Constantine is today perceived in the Revolutionary New Order. This "New Constantinianism" is the most recent version of settling for something less than the Kingdom of God.

In his classic *The Kingdom of God in America,* H. Richard Niebuhr scathingly criticized the ways in which an earlier "social gospel" movement had tried to make the Gospel of the Kingdom captive to partisan purpose. Then the partisan purpose was marked by complacent confidence in the inevitable triumph of the "progress" of Western civilization. But "triumphalism" cuts several ways, as Niebuhr well understood. Christian triumphalists have often dreamed of the triumph of the Church itself—resulting in a Christian, or a Catholic, or a Puritan society. Perhaps as often, triumphalism has taken the form of investing the Church's capital in what is deemed to be the wave of the future. A Church that no longer can call the plays insures its future by joining, by "making a contribution to," the winning side. Of those who settle for less than the Kingdom, Niebuhr wrote: "They sought to prove [the Gospel's] usefulness in promoting the dominant purposes of the age or group in which they lived, the purposes of nationalism where nationalism was in power, of capitalism where capitalism reigned, of radicalism where radicalism took the initiative."

What is at stake—in the fourth century, the twelfth century, and until the Kingdom comes—is the integrity of the Gospel. The Church, which is to proclaim and symbolize that Gospel, is inescapably engaged in the political and social orders of its time; the question is not whether but *how* the Church is engaged. Jesus declared that his disciples should be in but not of the world (John 17:16), a trick that Christians have never learned very well. Once we get the hang of living that way in one situation, the circumstances change, and we have to start learning all over again.

This book criticizes certain "radical" accommodations to the world. In truth, the radicalism is not very radical at all. Within the history of Christian betrayals of the true radicalness of the Gospel of the Kingdom, the current accommodation is depressingly conventional. Wearied of wandering and waiting upon the promise, we long for the fleshpots of Egypt. In this case, the fleshpots offer not physical sustenance so much as a cause, a movement, a struggle that gives us a feeling of importance and usefulness in the real world. When we are no longer sure that the Gospel is true we are eager to prove it is useful. And so, in the name of Christian discipleship, we end up subscribing to one of the great heresies of the modern world, the heresy that utility is the measure of truth.

A concluding caution: No doubt most Christians in this country and elsewhere reject the identification of the Gospel with Marxist and quasi-Marxist liberationism. Their rejection is of little religious significance, however, if it is derived only from their attachment to other social and political securities. This book will serve a very limited and not very interesting purpose if it merely advances one political agenda while opposing another. The more ambitious purpose, as I understand it, is to get us to think anew about how the Church ought to be in the world. The outcome of that could be a revivified ecumenical vision of a community of transcendent faith embracing those who espouse different and even conflicting views of our mundane tasks, including our political tasks. Pointing beyond all the political options of the present age, such a reconciled and reconciling Church would signal more believably the genuinely New Politics of the Kingdom of God.

Publisher's Note

"IN SEEKING TO EXTEND THEIR POWER beyond religious matters, [clergy] incur a risk of not being believed at all," wrote the nineteenth-century French commentator on America, Alexis de Tocqueville. "I am so much alive to the almost inevitable dangers which beset religious belief whenever the clergy take part in political affairs, and I am so convinced that Christianity must be maintained at any cost in the bosom of modern democracies, that I had rather shut up the priesthood within the sanctuary than allow them to step beyond it" (*Democracy in America*).

A century and a half later, Pope John Paul II has made it clear that he too is acutely aware that the clergy's involvement in politics can endanger the primary mission of Christianity. He expressed this concern in his address at the conference of Latin American bishops in Puebla, Mexico, in 1979, an address that is the centerpiece of this collection.

Early work in compiling the essays from which this book was drawn was done by Gary Potter, the president of Catholics for Christian Political Action, an independent national lay organization in Washington, D.C. Further selection was done by the editor of the volume, Quentin L. Quade, who is the executive vice-president of Marquette University in Milwaukee, Wisconsin. Dr. Quade, who has a Ph.D. from Notre Dame, has taught political science since 1959 and has long been concerned with the relation between ethics and politics. He wrote the introductions to the volume as a whole and to its four parts. Lutheran pastor and scholar Richard John Neuhaus, the author of the foreword, is a senior fellow of the Council on Religion and International Affairs.

As in all Center publications, the authors alone are responsible for the facts selected and the views expressed.

Washington, D.C.   ERNEST W. LEFEVER, President
May 1, 1982   Ethics and Public Policy Center

Introduction

By Quentin L. Quade

THROUGHOUT CHRISTIAN HISTORY, some Christians have sought to use religion for earthly ends—to invoke the sanction of the Church, the faith, or the Scriptures for particular political causes or systems. Others have viewed religion as something wholly above and beyond politics that cannot be joined to any particular cause.

What *should* be the relation of religion to politics? Specifically, how may the Catholic Church rightly influence particular political and economic issues? That is the essential question addressed in this volume. And the answer offered is: through believers acting as citizens. The Church may *not* be a direct political actor. Priests and other church leaders in their ecclesiastical capacity may not rightly act as politicians or political prophets. To do so is an unwarranted transfer of authority.

Some Catholic activists will insist that this position unduly limits the role of religion in politics. But it is the classic Catholic teaching. The Church must remain above politics, but its members may not escape their political responsibility as citizens. In more abstract terms, there are two autonomous but interacting realms, church and state, religion and the political order. Only when this is clearly understood can we avoid the twin pitfalls of pious irrelevance to or irresponsible involvement in the political drama of our age.

Two of the best commentators on the inclination to use religion for political ends are C. S. Lewis and Ronald Knox. Said the senior devil to the apprentice in the twenty-third of Lewis's *Screwtape Letters:*

> On the other hand we do want, and want very much, to make men treat Christianity as a means; preferably, of course, as a

means to their own advancement, but, failing that, as a means to anything—even to social justice. The thing to do is to get a man at first to value social justice as a thing the Enemy demands, and then work him on to the stage at which he values Christianity because it may produce social justice. For the Enemy will not be used as a convenience. . . . Fortunately, it is quite easy to coax humans around this little corner.

Jesus Christ, the scriptures that describe his earthly intervention, and the core tradition of his followers seem to agree with Screwtape. On a plain reading, they provide no warrant—no authority or reasonable grounds—for direct political use of Christ or his Church. Any who claim to find in Christ a platform for either political *action* or political *knowledge* must be asked to show their warrant. They must be asked to produce the chain of evidence and analysis that human beings normally insist upon in their endeavors.

Asked to show such a warrant, such people are likely to answer: the warrant is the zeal in my bosom. While one cannot deny the *possibility* that God truly speaks in such bosoms and through such zeal, one also cannot deny that if he does, he does so privately. Unless that private revelation can be communicated with intellectual integrity to others, it remains moot. In *Enthusiasm,* Ronald Knox emphasizes the intellectual element in moral concern:

> That there should be a few people, close friends of God, who seem to live by instinct and bypass calculation, is well enough; even the common run of us may experience, now and again, a flash of intuition which seemed akin to inspiration. But when a whole sect aspires to be spoon-fed with providential guidance, such as makes all deliberation, all effort of decision, henceforth unnecessary, there is ground for misgiving. Our mental powers also are from God.

Because "our mental powers also are from God," and because people should not be used, should not be manipulated, should not be tempted to follow without knowing why and where to, the person claiming Christ's warrant in politics must be asked to defend it in rational discourse.

If Lewis and Knox have alerted us to the activist tendency to overextend the mandate Christ gave us, others more recently have shown the problem in its more organized religious manifestations.

The Protestant version of this problem is set forth in Paul Ramsey's 1967 *Who Speaks for the Church?*, which comments on the political pretensions of the World Council of Churches' (WCC) Geneva Conference on Church and Society; Ernest W. Lefever's 1979 *Amsterdam to Nairobi,* which looks at the change in WCC political efforts from the end of World War II to 1979; and Edward Norman's 1979 *Christianity and the World Order,* the Reith Lectures for 1978, which rigorously examines a variety of organized efforts to do politics in Christ's name—without established authority. These three volumes make it clear that the Catholic political excesses to be discussed in this volume can hardly claim novelty as a virtue.

Modern Catholic efforts to use Christ politically had until recently been relatively well contained by what I will call the mainstream of Catholic social teaching. This body of mainstream teaching would include the social encyclicals from *Rerum Novarum* (1891) to *Pacem in Terris* (1963); the steady admonitions for peace of Benedict XV and Pius XII; the critique of Communism by Pius XI, *Divini Redemptoris* (1937); and, from the Second Vatican Council, the *Declaration on Religious Freedom* (*Dignitatis Humanae,* 1965) and, supremely, the *Pastoral Constitution on the Church in the Modern World* (*Gaudium et Spes,* 1965), in which the bishops of Vatican II pulled together the whole of formal teaching on social and political matters. The mainstream therefore takes in the period from 1891 to 1965. A later document that is in stride with these is Pope Paul VI's Apostolic Letter of May 14, 1971, *Octogesima Adveniens (Observing the Eightieth Anniversary of 'Rerum Novarum').*

These various teachings deal with a multitude of specific issues and set forth a multitude of relevant principles. For example, *Rerum Novarum* and *Quadragesimo Anno* (1931) develop the doctrine of the social responsibilities inherent in property ownership: the common good must be served. And *Divini Redemptoris* dwells on the personalist perception of man, implicit in Christ's teachings, which cannot be reconciled with the man-as-mass of Marx and Lenin. But our concern here is not with the particular social teachings of these documents. Rather, it is with what the documents say or imply about the political capacity and competence of the Church and churchmen.

In his preface to a collection of the major social teachings of the Catholic Church from 1891 to 1963 (*The Social Teachings of the Church,* edited by Anne Fremantle), Ivan Illich wrote, "These encyclicals . . . outline principles. . . . They are neither cookbooks nor collections of laws: they do not . . . lay down technical and detailed norms of behavior." That accurately characterizes the pre-Vatican II social commentaries. These greatly interesting documents, often marked by powerful analysis and intellectual integrity, are very careful to avoid any suggestion that the *disposition* to serve the human good is tantamount to *knowledge* of the human good.

Vatican II's *Pastoral Constitution on the Church in the Modern World* is usually referred to as ground-breaking. It has always seemed to me to be instead a very intelligently done synthesis of traditional understandings. Certainly it was traditional in what it said about the Church and political action. For instance: "The role and competence of the Church being what it is, she must in no way be confused with the political community, nor bound to any political system" (section 76). And: "The Church guards the heritage of God's Word and draws from it religious and moral principles, without always having at hand the solution to particular problems. She desires thereby to add the light of revealed truth to mankind's store of experience. . ." (33). Such passages show an appropriate modesty, and a careful understanding of how the Church, that great teacher of values and principles, informs social judgment but is not responsible for it. That insight is crystal clear in this passage:

> Often enough the Christian view of things will itself suggest some specific solution in certain circumstances. Yet it happens rather frequently, and legitimately so, that with equal sincerity some of the faithful will disagree with others on a given matter. Even against the intentions of their proponents, however, solutions proposed on one side or another may be easily confused by many people with the Gospel message. Hence it is necessary for people to remember that no one is allowed in the aforementioned situations to appropriate the Church's authority for his opinion [43].

This view respects the contingencies under which actual decisions are made, recognizes the divisiveness that necessarily accompanies the political act, and asserts that the religious bond should not be subjected to that division.

In *Octogesima Adveniens,* the 1971 apostolic letter honoring the eightieth anniversary of *Rerum Novarum,* Pope Paul VI sought to bring up to date the major social teachings, including his own *Populorum Progressio* (1967). This 1971 statement is another that various commentators see as a substantial departure, and as perhaps a warrant for an extended political role for Church and believer. It really is not, though it suffers some ambiguities in this respect. Preponderantly, it is a *very* cautious and careful analysis of church thinking on many social issues. It stands in sharp contrast to *Populorum Progressio,* which, as we will see, is far more an invitation to political excess. Basically, in its admonitions and exhortations on specific social matters, this letter of 1971 claims to *know* less than *Populorum Progressio* explicitly or implicitly claims to know.

Of special interest in *Octogesima Adveniens* is Paul VI's approach to the question of warrants for political action by the Church or by anyone in its name. The document, though not free of ambiguity, clearly stands in the mainstream Catholic tradition of restraint and modesty. The Pope stresses that the concreteness and diversity in situations preclude universal pronouncements—and indeed, "such is not our ambition nor is it our mission" (4). The Gospel is "not out of date" and should provide guidelines and norms. "It is not however to be utilized for the profit of particular temporal options, to the neglect of its universal and eternal message." Later Paul VI gives almost a textbook illustration of why and how the Christ-inspired citizen should accept political responsibility; he is to perform his duty without *hubris,* without pride or arrogance (46). And the Pope asserts: "In concrete situations, and taking account of solidarity in each person's life, one must recognize a legitimate variety of possible options. The same Christian faith can lead to different commitments" (50).

What I here described as the mainstream of post-1891 Catholic teaching on the Church's political competence calls for:

1. Modesty or caution about any capacity to know what right political action is on the basis of religious perception alone.

2. Care in the terminology used when one is exhorting and prescribing.

3. Rigor in respecting the essential difference between Church and state as human institutions.

These characteristics reflect a moral sense of the uniqueness of political action, of the need to bring principles to bear in circumstances that cannot be known *a priori*. The mainstream teachings reject the idea of a religious warrant enabling the Church or any churchman to claim political pertinence in specific matters on religious grounds. Yet, while denying such a warrant, they make clear the Church's legitimate concern for human welfare. This concern, shared by the state, produces the Church-state overlap of interests that, in careless hands, can produce a conflict between the two orders. The mainstream teachings do not justify such a conflict.

But between the end of Vatican II in 1965 and John Paul II's address to Latin American bishops at Puebla, Mexico, in 1979, a substantial drift developed in basic church teaching on religion and politics. Pope Paul VI's *Populorum Progressio* is considered by many a turning point at which the forces created by Vatican II moved from relatively traditional paths to more "radically" politicized ones. This reading seems plausible to me. The date of the document (March 1967) fits the theory, and the continual uses and abuses of it in subsequent church literature suggest that it was indeed pivotal. Yet an important point should be made: if *Populorum Progressio* contributed to the development of political pretensions in the Church's name, the reason was not that it made any overt claim to a political capacity. It is quite restrained in this respect; for example: "Experienced in human affairs, the Church, without attempting to interfere in any way in the politics of states," seeks only the "kingdom of heaven" and "not to conquer any earthly power" (13).

How then does *Populorum Progressio* violate the mainstream? It does so in the *knowledge* it claims, the specificity and competence it asserts in concrete matters. It does not acknowledge that people of equal virtue may hold contrary judgments in the realms of politics and economics. Moreover, in addition to this repeated simplism about economic and political matters, it resorts regularly to "purple passages" that, though they may make the heart beat faster and the passions rise, will not do much to promote actual understanding. Consider this: "But humanity is advancing along the path of history like the waves of a rising tide encroaching gradually on the shore" (17). Are we going somewhere *inevitably,* and is the somewhere inevitably *upward,* and is mankind making this journey or are *men* doing so?

The tendency is even better seen in this interesting juxtaposition. Paul VI says: "Today the peoples in hunger are making a dramatic appeal to the peoples blessed with abundance. The Church shudders at the cry of anguish and calls each one to give a loving response of charity to this brother's cry for help" (3). That seems a warranted exhortation, a legitimate application of "feed the hungry, clothe the naked" to contemporary circumstances. But two paragraphs later Paul VI describes his creation of the Pontifical Commission on Justice and Peace, which, he says, is ordained to bring "to the whole of God's people the full knowledge of the part expected of them at the present time, so as to further the progress of poorer peoples, encourage social justice among nations, and offer to less developed nations *the means whereby they can further their own progress"* (italics added). This rather clearly leaps from the general to the particular—offering "means"—without any acknowledgment that many different "means" might lead to such progress, or that such a leap presupposes a vast number of specialized skills.

The Paulist Press in 1967 published a translation of *Populorum Progressio* with an extensive introduction and commentary by the renowned economist Barbara Ward. The form and tone of Miss Ward's comments illustrate the point that the document seems to oversimplify what is inherently complex, and to invite an exaggerated interpretation of what one can know from religion's revelation alone. She sees in the encyclical a new "note of crisis and urgency." "The Pope speaks of the 'intolerable public scandal' of preferring 'national or personal ostentation' to the needs of the poor." She comments, "He speaks, in prophetic anger, . . . and warns the rich that 'continued greed will certainly call down upon them the judgment of God and the wrath of the poor.' " Miss Ward was impressed, apparently, by a rhetorical passion that offers no demonstration of its accuracy or germaneness. How does one conclude that failure to meet the needs of the poor derives from "ostentation" rather than from, for example, ignorance of how to meet those needs, or the inadequacies of indigenous leadership? How do we move from *systemic* problems of world development to allegations of *personal* vices such as "greed"? How does one conclude *a priori* that the productivity of one segment has been bought at another's expense when it might, in fact, be nothing more than a matter of historical circumstance?

Populorum Progressio invites the removal of distinctions and obliterates the intermediate steps that good judgment demands. It does these things in such a way as to suggest to anyone who wants to hear that somehow the right religious spirit, expressed with sufficient passion, is the essence of prudent political action, rather than just one prelude to such action.

On November 30, 1971, the Synod of Bishops, Second General Assembly, released a document entitled *Justice in the World*. If *Populorum Progressio* started the serious breaching of the mainstream teaching, *Justice in the World* is probably its most prominent successor. This document provides clear support for the view that political knowledge and the capacity for political action reside in the Church. Yet the bishops, after gazing into the political abyss, abruptly pull far back from it.

Let us look first at how close the bishops got to the abyss. They tell us that they "have noted the inmost stirring moving the world in its depths" (4) and hear "the appeal of a world that by its perversity contradicts the plan of its Creator" (5). They can see that "the hopes and forces which are moving in the world in its very foundations are not foreign to the dynamism of the Gospel" (5), even as they are aware that "the uncertainty of history and the painful convergences in the ascending path of the human community direct us to sacred history" (6).

How one reconciles in adjoining paragraphs the "ascending path" with the fact that "the world in which the Church lives and acts is held captive by a tremendous paradox" (7) is not made clear. This document shows little sense of obligation to be reasonable, cautious, analytic, and bound by evidence. It does not distinguish between the Church as the City of God and politics as an art and practice in the worldly city. These flaws invite a too-easy presumption of political relevance.

The problems of *Justice in the World* can be portrayed much more directly. In sacred history "God has revealed himself to us, and made known to us, as it is brought progressively to realization, his plan of liberation and salvation which is once and for all fulfilled in the Paschal Mystery of Christ" (6). What can this "liberation" mean? In a literal sense from a Christian perspective, it would probably have to mean "you'll get your reward in heaven"—the very opiate railed against by Feuerbach, Marx, and others. But the bishops have another intention: "Action on behalf of justice and participation in the transformation of the world fully appear to us as a constitutive dimension of the preaching of the Gospel, or, in other words, of the Church's mission for the redemption of the human race and its liberation from every oppressive situation" (6).

"Action" in the political order is part of the Church's mission? *Every* oppressive human situation is to be cleansed by such action? That seems to be the point, utopian and intrusive though it may be. In no way do such avowals prepare the reader for the retreat to come: "Of itself it does not belong to the Church, insofar as she is a religious and hierarchical community, to offer concrete solutions in the social, economic and political spheres for justice in the world" (37). And if the seemingly expansive, politicizing view of the Church's competence needs any further assault, consider this: "Christians' specific contribution to justice is the day-to-day life of the individual believer acting like the leaven of the Gospel in his family, his school, his work, and his social and civic life" (49). That puts the bishops right back in the mainstream with its emphasis on personal responsibility rather than institutional involvement. *Justice in the World,* then, does not actually claim to provide a political warrant, but it certainly provides a temptation for the Church to meddle in politics.

Three and one-half years later, the same Synod of Bishops in its

Third General Assembly promulgated *Evangelization of the Modern World*. This document is repeatedly cited as authorizing a political life for the Church and for believers in the name of the Church. It really does not claim to provide such authority, but it *is* ambiguous on the point.

The following passages from this document deserve careful scrutiny. "Among the many subjects dealt with by the Synod, special attention was drawn to the mutual relationships between evangelization [on the one hand] and integral salvation or the complete liberation of man and of peoples [on the other]" (12). What do these words mean? The usual meanings of "evangelization," "salvation," and "liberation" do not suggest the kind of relationship this paragraph implies. But no clarification is offered. Instead, the very next sentence, perhaps in the belief that repetition will work when argument is not available, asserts that the bishops "experienced profound unity in reaffirming the intimate connection between evangelization and liberation." What exactly *is* that connection? Perhaps the bishops cannot answer that question, but "let us nurture the hope that the Church, in more faithfully fulfilling the work of evangelization, will announce the total salvation of man, or rather his complete liberation, and from now on will start to bring this about" (12). And to round the circle once again, the bishops assure us that the Church will lead us "toward freedom under all its forms—liberation from sin, from individual or collective selfishness—and to full communion with God and with men who are like brothers" (12).

On the matter of the Church and political action, then, there has been a drift away from the Catholic mainstream. Both growing out of and contributing to this drift during the last fifteen years is a collection of emphases known as "liberation theology." The term does not have a clear single meaning, but its roots can be found in the political theological writings of European Catholics like Karl Rahner, Jürgen Moltmann, and Johannes Metz. Its major flowering, theoretically and practically, has been in Latin America, in the words and deeds of such persons as Juan Luis Segundo, Helder Camara, and Gustavo Gutiérrez.

This volume will not provide a general survey of that literature.

Rather, it will offer an excellent summary of liberation theology in a major Gutiérrez essay. Then, against the mainstream of Catholic background discussed above, it will analyze some of the implications of the liberationist position. Next it will present Pope John Paul II's Puebla critique of the type of social-political religion advocated by liberation theology. It will develop some of the implications of John Paul's teaching, and note the efforts of many to avoid or redefine those implications. Finally, it will then look at the Pope's very clear reiterations of his positions in Africa and Brazil, which can leave little doubt that whatever authority a Catholic liberationist may claim for his theology, it *cannot* be the authority of the Church of the Pope.

The purpose of this book, then, is to clarify some of the often cloudy political argument now going on in the Catholic Church. When the clouds have cleared, this central fact should be apparent: liberation theology and its cousins are not religion but politics, a series of programs for the economic and political redemption of society. The proponents of these programs invoke the authority of Christ rather than defending their positions in the political area as the simply political platforms that they are.

I trust that this volume will reinforce a basic principle: Call things by their right names. Use things for what they are intended. Truth, justice, and freedom demand no less.

PART ONE

Prelude to Puebla

The Christian tradition yields a core of human values and ends that should provide for believers as citizens the basis for an enlightened public policy. The Christian ethic carries the obligation to seek the values it proclaims. But it does not yield specifics of the political process nor the precise answers to particular public problems.

Politics is precisely the specifying of social alternatives and the choosing among them in response to complicated social demands and objectives. In such choosing, politics is inevitably divisive and partial. But an enlightened polity seeks to harmonize conflicting values, to synthesize them, to ensure—insofar as possible—that the "choosing among" does not involve destruction of the interests of those whose preferences do not prevail.

In the hurly-burly of politics, we see little of the pristine and the abstractly pure that we associate with religious values. That is not because such values are irrelevant to politics, nor because politics is value-free. Rather, it is because the political process and its central actions consist of values-in-conflict in a particular time and place, rather than simply values or principles in themselves. The political act, like every moral act, is always unique, always a response to circumstance, and always influenced by the values that motivate the actor, whether an individual or a government.

This understanding of politics enables us to see the limitations of the Church as a political actor. The Gospel points to desirable human ends—freedom, justice, love, compassion. It creates an obligation and a disposition to seek these ends. But the Gospel does not provide a political guidebook. It does not tell a congressman how to vote on the Panama Canal issue or what to do

13

about the neutron bomb. It does not endorse any political systems but provides the basis for judging all systems and their acts. And it does not give any assurance of perfection in this life and in this world.

Gustavo Gutiérrez is a leading exponent of liberation theology. What do we find in his essay in this section? Basically, Gutiérrez is a utopian; he believes man can make heaven on earth. He traces sin and evil to systems, not to human nature, and appears to believe that greed began with capitalism and will end with its demise.

Gutiérrez moves easily from the Gospel's concern for the poor to specific political solutions: the poor "are the oppressed, the exploited, the workers cheated of the fruits of their work, stripped of their being as men. The poverty of the poor is not therefore an appeal for generous action to relieve it, but a demand for the construction of a different social order." A vast distance separates these two kinds of observations, that the Gospel teaches compassion for the poor and that compassion demands "the construction of a different social order." But the two are presented as equally derived from the Christian faith. Apparently Father Gutiérrez feels no obligation to explain how he knows political things—e.g., that it is time for radical change, or what a new and better order consists of and how it can be achieved. Addressing particular issues and structures, he offers no more defense than that "we are in the presence of what is necessarily an offshoot of the Gospel."

Gutiérrez resorts to a standard defense of undue religious intrusion in politics when he says his work cannot be condemned for going beyond gospel warrant because it is not "partisan." Such a statement—which appears routinely in European and Latin American liberationist literature—betrays at the very least a drastic failure of political understanding. Politics is the assigning of social priorities from among competing options. It is therefore *necessarily* divisive. Partisanship and parties are only methods to articulate the options. To say one avoids the pitfall of religious overextension by remaining nonpartisan reflects a profound misunderstanding of politics.

This blurred political vision is evident also when Gutiérrez describes the Church as the flock, the people, rather than as the hierarchy, and at the same time talks of the Church as a unitary agency for political purposes. If the Church is the hierarchy, it can have a unitary but drastically limited political role: teacher. If the Church is the people, it can have a comprehensive political role, obviously—but certainly not a unitary one. To think of the Church both as the people and as a united organization for political purposes is to engage in a utopian dream that diminishes the freedom of believers who have different visions.

In the second essay in this section, Dale Vree examines Gutiérrez's major work, *A Theology of Liberation*. Vree points to what seems to be Gutiérrez's conclusion: the Kingdom equals liberation equals revolution equals Marxist analysis equals Christlikeness. Vree concludes that liberation theology, as represented in Gutiérrez's work, clothes politics in the garments of religion.

It is important to note the limited effect of finding religion's limits. We cannot, for example, conclude "no more revolution, revolution no more" from the simple fact that religion does not contain a political program. The question of when and whether revolution is an acceptable instrument requires its own analysis. Similarly, it is not possible to determine *a priori* the form of revolutionary activity that might be called for in a given society. It *is* possible, however, to attack any utopian presumption surrounding revolutionary activity, for history gives no warrant for optimism. And it is possible to say with certainty that revolutionary activity properly dubbed Marxist-Leninist has been hugely destructive of human life and spirit, and that it is antithetical to anything like Christian personalism.

GUSTAVO GUTIERREZ

Liberation, Theology, and Proclamation

THEOLOGY IS AN UNDERSTANDING of the faith and a re-reading of the Word as it is lived in the Christian community. The ensuing reflection is oriented towards the communication of the faith and the proclamation of the good news of the Father's love for all men. To evangelize is to witness to that love and say it is revealed to us and made flesh in Christ.

The basis for discourse about the faith is midway between experience and communication. Theology is concerned with our being as men and as Christians, and is a function of the proclamation of the Good News. That is why it is a permanent yet ever-changing task. We have to get on with *being* Christians within an historical process that is transforming the conditions of human life all the time.The Gospel must be proclaimed to men who realize themselves as they work out their own destiny. Theological discourse concerns a Truth that is the Way; it is about a Word that is located in the midst of history. A task for all times, theology assumes different forms, depending on the Christian experience and the

Gustavo Gutiérrez, a Peruvian priest, is one of the foremost proponents of liberation theology. This essay distills the essence of his influential book "A Theology of Liberation" (1973). The essay appeared in "The Mystical and Political Dimension of the Christian Faith," Concilium 96, edited by Gutiérrez and Claude Geffré (New York: Herder and Herder, 1974). It is reprinted by permission of T. and T. Clark, Publishers, Edinburgh, Scotland.

17

proclamation of the Gospel to men at a given moment of historical development.

⸶ Recent years in Latin America have been marked by the real, demanding discovery of the world of the other: the poor, the marginal, exploited class of society. In a social order which in terms of economics, politics, and ideology was made by a few for their own benefit, the "others," that is, exploited lower classes, oppressed cultures, races subject to discrimination, are beginning to make their own voices heard. They are beginning to speak out directly and less and less through intermediaries, to rediscover themselves and make their presence felt in the system. They are increasingly less inclined to submit to demagogic manipulation or more or less disguised social assistance; instead they are gradually becoming the subjects of their own history and are forging a radically different society.

They can discover this only from within the historical process of liberation, which seeks to build a truly egalitarian, fraternal, and just society. For some time now, a growing number of Christians have been sharing in the process of liberation, and through it, in the discovery of the world of the exploited and peripheral people of the South American continent. This commitment gives rise to a new way of being a man and a believer, of living and thinking the faith, of being called together in an "ecclesia."

This sharing of Christians in the process of liberation varies in radicalism and is virtually a process of searching and advancing "by trial and error." At times it gets bogged down at difficult points in the road, at others it moves forward at speed, thanks to some event or other. But it is following a path whose new significance for theological reflection and for the celebration in community of the faith is gradually becoming clear.

In this article I want to make a few observations about a theological task which begins from an historical practice of liberation, through which the poor and oppressed of this world are endeavoring to build a different social order and a new way of being men. This theological reflection is impelled by a desire to speak the word of the Lord to all men from that position of solidarity.

The irruption of the other, the poor man, into our lives leads to active solidarity with his interests and his struggles. This commitment is expressed in an attempt to transform a social order which breeds marginalization and oppression. Participation in the historical practice of liberation is ultimately the practice of love, the love of Christ in one's neighbor; and of encounter with the Lord in the midst of a conflictual history.

Rediscovering the other means entering his own world. It also means a break with ours. The world of inward-looking absorption with self, the world of the "old man," is not only interior but socio-culturally conditioned. To enter the world of the other, the poor man, with the actual demands involved, is to begin to be a "new man." It is a process of conversion.

Love for one's neighbor is an essential component of Christian existence. But as long as I consider as my neighbor the man "near me," the one I meet on *my* way, the one who comes to me seeking aid ("Who is *my* neighbor?"), my world remains the same. All individual gestures of aid, all superficial reform of society is a love that stays comfortably at home ("If they love those who love them, what reward will they have?"). If, on the other hand, I consider my neighbor as the man in *whose* path I deliberately place myself, the man "distant" from me, the one whom I approach ("Which of these three was neighbor *to this man?*"), if I make myself the neighbor of the man I seek out in streets and squares, in factories and marginal *barrios,* in the fields and the mines, my world changes.

That is what happens when an authentic and effective "option for the poor" is made, because for the Gospel, the poor man is the neighbor *par excellence.* This option is the axle on which turns a new way of being a man and being a Christian in Latin America.[1] But the "poor" do not exist as an act of destiny; their existence is not politically neutral or ethically innocent. The poor are a by-product of the system in which we live and for which we are responsible. The poor are marginalized in our social and cultural world. They are the oppressed, the exploited, the workers cheated of the fruits of their work, stripped of their being as men. The poverty of the poor is not therefore an appeal for generous action, but a demand for the construction of a different social order.

It is, however, necessary to take one more step. The option for the poor and the oppressed through a liberating commitment leads to the realization that this commitment cannot be isolated from the social set-up to which they belong; otherwise we would not go beyond "being sorry for the situation." The poor, the oppressed, are members of a culture which is not respected, a race which is discriminated against, a social class subtly or openly exploited by another social class. To opt for the poor is to opt for the marginalized and exploited, to take stock of the social conflict and side with the dispossessed. To opt for the poor is to enter the world of the oppressed race, culture, and social class, to enter the universe of their values and cultural categories. This means solidarity with their interests and their struggles.

The poor man is therefore someone who questions the ruling social order. Solidarity with the poor means taking stock of the injustice on which this order is built, and of the countless means it employs to maintain itself. It also means understanding that one cannot be *for* the poor and oppressed if one is not *against* all that gives rise to man's exploitation of man. For this same reason, solidarity cannot limit itself to just saying no to the way things are arranged. It must be more than that. It must be an effort to forge a society in which the worker is not subordinated to the owner of the means of production, a society in which the assumption of social responsibility for political affairs will include social responsibility for real liberty and will lead to the emergence of a new social consciousness.

Solidarity with the poor implies the transformation of the existing social order. It implies a liberating social praxis: that is, a transforming activity directed towards the creation of a just, free society.*

During the last two centuries man has begun to realize his capacity to transform swiftly and in a controlled manner the world in which he lives. That experience has changed the course of history and gives a definitive character to our age. Unsuspected

---

Praxis, from the Greek word meaning "to do," means action or practice. "The Marxian concept of *praxis*," says Edward Norman in *Christianity and the World Order*, is "the involvement of the oppressed in the historical process of change."—ED.

possibilities have opened up for man's life on earth, but their appropriation for the benefit of a minority of the human race has provoked the frustration and exasperation of the dispossessed masses.

Throwing Off Nature's Constraints

The industrial revolution, as it was called, meant the beginning of a stage of broad and rapid production of consumer goods for man, based on a capacity to transform nature hitherto unknown.[2] The use of experimental science had already set in motion the attempt to dominate nature, but this mastery was only to reach full consciousness and maturity when scientific knowledge was translated into a technique of manipulation of the material world, and into the possibility of satisfying the vital needs of man on a large scale.[3] The productive powers of man increased beyond foreseeable limits and brought about a revolutionary change in the economic activity of society. The process has continued, and advances spirally, and we are today in the middle of what is called a second industrial revolution. All this has given contemporary man the consciousness that he is capable of modifying his living conditions radically, and has given a clear and stimulating affirmation of his freedom vis-à-vis Nature. It has also produced the widest-ranging differences among the peoples of the earth that history has ever known.

One of the most uncontrolled consequences of the industrial revolution was the progressive displacement of man by the machine. This created a marginal social surplus in the course of the production of wealth: the so-called reserve industrial pool consisting of a growing mass of marginalized people not reabsorbed by the system. The nineteenth century was slow to take account of this social price for the accelerated rhythm of industrialization and its corresponding technological boom. Furthermore, as technical progress became more and more refined, and the standard of living of the developed countries rose, the process was accompanied by an international division of labor which produced those vast differences between one country and another.

Therefore, whereas the industrial revolution has given modern man a unique situation and power to transform nature, it has also sharpened contradictions in society until a situation of international crisis has been reached which forceful measures can no longer hide.

These consequences of the industrial revolution make for a better understanding of the extent of another historical process, whose origins go back to the same period and give evidence of another aspect of man's transforming action. We refer to the political field, which experienced in the French Revolution the practical working of the possibility of a profound transformation in the existing social order. It declared the right of every man to share in the conduct of the society to which he belongs. Neither the immediate results of the French Revolution nor the largely declaratory character of that proclamation are our concern here. The important thing to note is that, with all its ambiguities, that event put an end to one kind of society, and from then on the people as a whole aspired to share in political power effectively and adopt an active role in history: in short, they aspired towards a truly democratic society. As in the previous instance, we are faced here with a new affirmation of man's freedom, this time in relation to social organization. But for the democratic organization of society to be real it is assumed that just economic conditions exist; if these do not exist, explosive tensions occur.

The contemporaries of those events in their opening stages were acutely conscious of being on the threshold of a new historical era marked by critical reason and man's transforming liberty.[4] All this was to lead, they thought, to a different man, more master of himself, and of his destiny in history. History could no longer be thought of with nature divorced from society. The industrial revolution and the political revolution were in fact to appear more and more clearly, not as two processes which happened to be contemporary or convergent, but as two movements depending one on the other. As both advanced, their reciprocal involvement became more evident. To transform history required a simultaneous transformation in nature and society. In this transforming praxis, there is more than a new consciousness of the meaning of economic and political action—there is a new way of being man in history.

To speak of a transformation of history from the standpoint of dominated countries and marginalized men, the poor of this world, leads us to see this as a liberating praxis. This means seeing in it something which is perhaps missed when it is viewed from the standpoint of the minority of the human race, who control the major part of scientific and technical assets and also political power in the world today. That is why a liberating praxis has a subversive look about it: that is only natural, in a social order where the poor man, the "other" of this society, is only just beginning to be listened to.[5]

What is really at stake is not a greater rationalization of economic activity or a better social organization, but through them the whole question of justice and love. The terms are classical and perhaps little used in strictly political language, but they recall for us the human reality at the heart of the matter. They remind us that we are speaking of men, of whole peoples who are suffering poverty and despoliation, who cannot exercise the most elementary human rights, who scarcely know they are men.

That is why a liberating praxis, in so far as it starts from authentic solidarity with the poor and the oppressed, is specifically a practice of love: real love, effective and historical, for men of flesh and blood. Then love of our neighbor is love of Christ, who is identified with the very least of our brothers. Any attempt to separate the love of God from the love of our neighbor gives rise to attitudes which impoverish the one or the other. It is easy to set a "praxis of heaven" against a "praxis of earth" and vice versa: easy, but not in accord with the Gospel of God made man. Therefore it seems more genuine and profound to speak of a practice of love which is rooted in the gratuitous, free love of the Father, and which makes itself history in solidarity with the poor and dispossessed, and through them in solidarity with all men.

Believing and Understanding

Commitment to the process of liberation, with all its political demands, means taking on the world of the poor and the oppressed in a real and effective manner. This sets up a new spiritual requirement at the very heart of the liberating praxis. I mean the matrix of a new theological reflection, of an intellection of the Word, the free gift of God, breaking into human existence and transforming it.

The praxis of liberation must lead one to become poor with the poor. For the Christian committed to it, this will be a way of identifying oneself with Christ, who came into the world to proclaim the Gospel to the poor and liberate the oppressed. Evangelical poverty thus began to be lived as an act of liberation and love towards the poor of this world, as solidarity with them and protest against the poverty in which they live; as identification with the interests of the oppressed classes and a rejection of the exploitation of which they are the victims.

If the ultimate cause of the exploitation and alienation of man is egotism, the underlying motive of voluntary poverty is love for one's neighbor. Poverty—the results of social injustice, which has its deepest roots in sin—is accepted not in order to make it an ideal of life, but in order to witness to the evil it represents. The condition of the sinner, and its consequences, were accepted by Christ, not to idealize them, but out of love and solidarity with men, and to redeem them from sin; to fight against human egotism and abolish all injustice and division among men. Consequently, the witness of poverty lived as an authentic imitation of Christ, instead of separating us from the world, places us at the very heart of the situation of despoilment and oppression, and from there proclaims liberation and full communion with the Lord. Spiritual poverty is proclaimed and lived as a way of being totally at God's disposal, as a spiritual childhood.[6]

All this means entering a different world and outlines a Christian experience as yet untried, full of possibilities and promise, but with no lack of twists and blind alleys on the route ahead. There is no smooth, triumphant highway for the life of faith. Absorption in the political demands of a liberating commitment can lead to difficulties. The tensions of living in solidarity with exploited people who belong to a Church containing many members on the side of the prevailing social order, can cause some to lose the dynamism of their faith and suffer the anguish of a dichotomy between their Christian existence and their political action.

Crueler still is the case of those who see their love for God vanish in favor of a love which he himself has inspired and nourished; the love of man, a love which, unable to observe the unity demanded by the Gospel, remains heedless of the plenitude God contains in himself.

Such cases exist. To be present in the frontier areas of the Christian community, where the revolutionary commitment is at its most intense, is not a tranquil experience. The clues to any solution can arise only from the depths of the problem itself. Protective measures conceal reality and delay any useful response. They also display a neglect of the urgency and gravity of the reasons which lead to a commitment to men exploited by a cruel, impersonal system, and finally they show a lack of belief in the strength of the Gospel and of faith.

In reality a liberating commitment now means for many Christians an authentic *spiritual experience,* in the original, biblical sense of the term; a living in the Spirit which makes us recognize ourselves as freely and creatively sons of the Father and brothers of man ("God has sent into our hearts the Spirit of the Son who proclaims Abba, Father"). In Christ we become simultaneously and inseparably sons and brothers ("Whoever sees me sees the Father; whoever does the will of my Father, he is my brother"). Only through concrete acts of love and solidarity will our encounter be effective with the poor, with the exploited man, and in him our encounter with Christ (". . . you gave it to me"). Our denial of love and solidarity will be a rejection of Christ (". . . you refused it to me"). The poor man, the other, reveals the totally Other to us.

This is what is involved, life in a presence of the Lord, at the center of an activity in one way or another related to the political world, with its confrontation of interests and conflicts and the need for a level of scientific rationale to understand it in its complexity. To paraphrase a well-known saying, we need "contemplatives in political action." We are unused to this. A spiritual experience seems to us something encountered well away from human realities of such marked lack of purity as political action. The specific form of our insertion in the realities of politics will depend on our situation in society and in the church community. However, that is where we are going, towards an encounter with the Lord not in the poor man "isolated and good," but in the oppressed man, fighting ardently for his most elementary rights and for the construction of a society in which men can live as men. History is the scene of the revelation God makes of the mystery of his person. His word reaches us in the measure of our involvement in the evolution of history.

To opt for the poor man, to be identified with his lot, to share his destiny, means a desire to make of history genuine brotherhood for all men. It means accepting the free gift of sonship and opting for the cross of Christ in the hope and joy of his Resurrection.

In these concrete conditions the process of conversion occurs, the nodal point of all spirituality. Conversion means going out of oneself, being open to God and others; it implies a break, but above all it means following a new path.[7] For that very reason, it is not an inward-looking, private attitude, but a process which occurs in the socio-economic, political, and cultural medium in which life goes on, and which is to be transformed. The encounter with Christ in the poor man constitutes an authentic spiritual experience. It is a living in the Spirit, the bond of love between Father and Son, God and man, man and man. Christians committed to an historical praxis of liberation try to live this kind of profound communion. They find the love of Christ in their encounter with the poor and in solidarity with them; they find faith in our situation as sons of the Father working for a society of brothers; and they find hope in the salvation of Christ, in commitment to the liberation of the oppressed.

All this is a unifying experience which all too often is impoverished when an attempt is made to express it. This may be due to its handling by theologians who tend to separate and even set at odds the elements of this experience; or it may be due to the defensive attitude adopted against Christian sectors who see in the commitment to liberation a challenge to their privileges in the present social order. The Christian experience involved is not without risk of being subject to *simpliste* identifications and distorting reductions; but it is a bold and profound attempt to live in

Christ by taking on oneself the history of suffering and injustice of the poor of this continent. To the extent that this experience has managed to achieve genuine expression and free itself from a mediatized language, its contribution has begun to show fertile possibilities for the whole ecclesial community.

Understanding Faith

At the root of all theology is the act of faith. It is not there as a simple intellectual adhesion to the message, but as a warm welcome of the gift of the Word heard in the ecclesial community; as an encounter with the Lord, as love for our brother. Faith concerns Christian existence taken as a whole. To welcome the Word, to make it life, a concrete act, is the starting-point for the intellection of faith. That is the meaning of St. Anselm's *"Credo ut intelligam,"* as he has expressed it in his celebrated text: "I do not try, O Lord, to penetrate your depths, because my intelligence could not conceivably attain that; but I wish to understand to some extent your truth, which my heart believes and loves. I do not seek to understand so as to believe, but *I believe in order to understand,* since I am sure that if I did not believe, I would not understand" (*Proslogium*, end of the first chapter).

The primacy of God and the grace of faith give theological work its *raison d'être*. Beginning from that, it can be properly grasped that if the Christian seeks to understand his faith it is ultimately as a function of the "imitation of Christ," which means thinking, feeling, and acting like him. An authentic theology is always a spiritual theology, as the Fathers understood it. The life of faith is not only the point of departure, it is also the point of arrival for the task which theology sets itself. Belief and understanding are part of a circle.

Theology always employs a certain rationale, even if it does not identify with it. This rationale corresponds to the cultural universe of the believer. Every theology asks itself about the meaning of the Word of God for us in the present in history, and attempts at a reply are made as a function of our culture and of the problems which face men of our time. From the standpoint of this cultural universe we reshape the message of the Gospel and the faith for our contemporaries and ourselves.

That is what Thomistic theology, for example, attempted, boldly using Aristotelian philosophy and the whole world vision to which it was tied. This was a step of first importance in the understanding of faith. Today we are witnessing a crisis in the rationale classically employed in theology. The matter has been amply studied and its causes precisely indicated, and no purpose would be served by going into further detail about it here. Among the results of this situation is the philosophical eclecticism which is one of the features of a certain contemporary philosophy. Another result is the efforts which we see, not so much to rebuild an impossible unitary theological system, but rather to find new ways towards the reformulation of the Word.[8] In a more radical manner perhaps, it has provoked questioning in the field of the theory of knowledge,[9] an area not perhaps given sufficient attention in theological thinking, but certainly requiring consideration. On what assumptions does theology base its approach to historical reality? What is the influence on our thological reflection of the place held by the ecclesial institution in present-day society? Or, to use a common expression nowadays, where does the theologian speak from? For what and for whom does he speak? These questions have opened a major consideration which always crops up when one stage is closing and another beginning: what is meant by making theology?

An important role in these queries is played by scientific knowledge, especially when history or psychology is touched upon. The sciences are forms of expression of human reason; they reveal to us aspects of nature and man which evade other approaches to these realities and therefore cannot be neglected by theology. Philosophical reflection, even when opening up new paths, preserves all its validity and is enriched in permanent dialogue with the sciences. It responds to questions which do not belong to the domain of the sciences, and it makes its own contribution to the knowledge of history and to the role of the free, creative action of man. This complexity and wide-ranging character of human knowledge is set to work in the historical praxis of liberation, and contributes to make it more effective. It is also present in any discourse on faith which is attempted from a position of solidarity with the poor and the marginalized.

Much contemporary theology seems to start from the challenge of the *non-believer*. He questions our *religious world* and faces it with a demand for profound purification and renewal. Bonhoeffer took up the challenge and put the incisive question which is at the root of many theological endeavors nowadays: how is God proclaimed in a world which has become adult? This challenge in a continent like Latin America does not come primarily from the man who does not believe, but from the *man who is not a man*, who is not recognized as such by the existing social order: he is in the ranks of the poor, the exploited; he is the man who is systematically and legally despoiled of his being as a man, who scarcely knows that he *is* a man. His challenge is not aimed first at our religious world, but at our *economic, social, political, and cultural world*; therefore it is an appeal for the revolutionary transformation of the very bases of a dehumanizing society.

The question is not therefore how to speak of God in an adult world, but how to proclaim him as a Father in a world that is not human. What is implied in telling this man who is not a man that he is a son of God? To some extent these were the questions put by Bartolomé de las Casas and many others in the sixteenth century on the basis of their encounter with the American natives. The discovery of the other, of the exploited, led to a reflection about the demands of faith which contrasted with that conducted by those who sided with the rulers, Ginés de Sepúlveda, for example.

Today the historical framework is different, the social analysis is another one, but we are witnessing the rediscovery of the poor man in Latin America. Solidarity with him means deliberate entry into the arena of history, into confrontation between countries and between social classes. It means entry on the side of the dominated and oppressed. However, the social system itself, which creates and justifies this situation, is not really questioned unless a share is taken in the efforts to transform it radically and forge a different order. Localization in the praxis of liberation means taking on what we called the complexity and wide-ranging character of human knowledge; ultimately it means entering a different cultural world.

From within this cultural world in which we are situated because of our involvement in the Latin American historical process, we try to reformulate the Gospel message. From this viewpoint discourse on faith will necessarily follow a different path from that presented to it when the challenge of the non-believer is taken as the starting-point. Theology will be a critical reflection from and about the historical praxis of liberation in confrontation with the Word of the Lord lived and accepted in faith. It will be a reflection in and about faith as a liberating praxis: an intellection of faith made from an option; a reflection based on a commitment to create a just, fraternal society, and with a duty to contribute to make that commitment fuller and more radical. The theological discourse becomes truth (is veri-fied) in its real, fecund insertion in the process of liberation.

To reflect on the faith as liberating practice is to reflect on a truth, which is made, and not just affirmed;[10] it is to start from a promise which is fulfilled throughout history and at the same time opens history up beyond itself. In the final instance the exegesis of the Word, to which theology wishes to contribute, is accomplished in deeds. This factor, not mere affirmations, will rescue the understanding of faith from idealism of whatever kind.

New Categories for Faith

Insertion in the liberating process constitutes a profound and decisive spiritual experience at the very heart of the historical commitment, with its necessary political implications. As we have already remarked, this is a source of knowledge and energy for a way of theologizing which opens up new perspectives.

We are not faced here with new fields of application of old theological notions, but with the provocation and necessity to live and think the faith in different socio-cultural categories. This has occurred at other times in the history of the Christian community and has always produced fears and anxieties. In this search, we are impelled by the urgency to pronounce the Word of the Lord in our everyday language.

This is the point at issue: a rereading of the Gospel message from

the standpoint of liberating practice. Theological discourse operates here as a mediator between a new manner of living the faith,
and its communication. If we accept that theology is a rereading of
the Gospel, this is carried out with a view to the proclamation of the
message.[11]

To know that the Lord loves us, to welcome the freè gift of his
love, is a profound source of joy for the man who lives by his Word.
To communicate that joy is to evangelize: it means communicating
the Good News of the love of God, which has changed our lives,
and communicating it freely, as the love which originated it was
freely given. The task of evangelization always starts from an
experience of the Lord: a living out of the love of the Father, who
makes us sons and transforms us by making us more fully men and
brothers of men.

To proclaim the Gospel is to proclaim the mystery of sonship and
brotherhood, a mystery hidden from all ages and now revealed in
Christ.[12] To proclaim the Gospel therefore means to call people
together in an "ecclesia," to unite them in an assembly. It is only in
a community that faith can be lived in love; only there can it be
celebrated and deepened; only there can it be lived in one single
gesture, as fidelity to the Lord and solidarity with all men. To
accept the Word is to convert the Other into others, the rest. We
live this Word with them. Faith cannot be lived on its private,
inward-looking plane because faith rejects all turning in upon
oneself. In the dynamism of the good news which reveals us as sons
of the Father and brothers one of another, is the creation of a
community, of the Church, which will be a visible sign before men
of liberation in Christ.

This proclamation of the Gospel calling us together in an
"ecclesia" is made from an option of real, active solidarity with the
interests and struggles of the poor, of the exploited classes. To try
to take up this "place" means a deep break with the way of living,
thinking, and communicating the faith in the Church of today. All
this demands a conversion to another world, a new style of intellection of the faith; and it leads to a reformulation of the message.[13]

In this reformation, what has come to be called the political
dimension of the Gospel takes on a new face. It is seen more clearly

than before that there is no question of adding on something from outside the Gospel by yielding to partisan pressures of our age, but that we are in the presence of what is necessarily an offshoot of the Gospel. Moreover, the political dimension is accepted frankly and openly. Its precise extent has still to be defined, and any simplistic view of it must be avoided, but no claim to be outside politics can obscure an evident reality or weaken a conviction that is growing firmer all the time. The gift of sonship is lived in history. By making men brothers, we welcome this gift, not in words but in deeds ("Not all who say to me Lord, Lord, will enter the Kingdom of Heaven, but he who does the will of my Father").

To struggle against all injustice, despoilment, and exploitation, to be committed to the creation of a more brotherly and human society, is to live the love of the Father, and witness to it. The proclamation of a God who loves all men equally must be given substance in history and must become history. To proclaim that love in a profoundly unequal society marked by injustice and the exploitation of some peoples by others, of one social class by another social class, will make this process of "becoming history" a conflict-laden, interpellating experience.

That is why we said that the political dimension is inside the dynamism of a Word which seeks to become incarnate in history. The demands of the Gospel are incompatible with the social situation which is being lived in Latin America, with the ways in which relations between men operate, with the structures in which these relations are found. More is required than the rejection of some individual injustice or other; we are faced with the need for a different social order. Only a certain degree of political maturity will permit a true political understanding of the Gospel and will prevent it from being reduced to an aid program, however sophisticated, or to a simple task of "human promotion." It will also avoid the reduction of the evangelizing task to a form of political action with its own laws and demands.

The authentic proclamation of the love of God, of brotherhood, and of the radical equality of all men, to the exploited man of our continent, will make him see that his situation is against the Gospel, and this will help him to take stock of the profound injustice of this state of affairs. The oppressed sectors will acquire a clear political consciousness only by direct participation in the struggles of the people; but in the complex totality of the political process which must break with an oppressive social order and lead to a brotherly society, the ideological struggle holds an important place. In Latin America, the whole "Christian set-up" is made to play a part inside the dominant ideology, which helps to strengthen and affirm a society divided into antagonistic classes. Conservative sectors in fact frequently appeal to Christian ideas to justify the social order which serves their interests and maintains their privileges. That is why the communication of the message reread from the standpoint of the other, of the poor and oppressed, will serve to unmask any attempt to ideologize the Gospel and justify a situation contrary to the most elemental demands of the Gospel.

The Danger of Reductionism

Are we faced with a political reductionism of the Gospel? While wishing to escape from one ideological use of Christianity, are we not falling into another? The danger exists, and it would be ingenuous and dishonest to deny it. It needs to be kept constantly in mind.

The rereading of the Gospel from the standpoint of solidarity with the poor and the oppressed enables us to condemn the way those in power fetter the Gospel in order to place it at the service of their own interests. We cannot do this properly, if we are not aware of the permanently creative and critical nature of the liberating message of the Gospel. This message is not identified with any social form, however just it may appear to us at the time. The word of the Lord interpellates every historical achievement and sites it within the broad perspective of the radical and total liberation of Christ, the Lord of history. A relapsing into ideology made to justify a particular social situation is inevitable when the Gospel is not lived as the word of a Father who loves us freely and gratuitously, with a love which renews the face of the earth, and calls us always to a new life in his Son.

The liberation of Christ is not reduced to a religious plane tangential to the concrete world of men, as those who wish to domesticate the Gospel claim. The salvation of Christ is in fact so full that nothing escapes it. Evangelization is liberating because it is a message of total liberation which necessarily includes a demand for the transformation of the historical and political conditions in which men live. But this is only to be grasped in all its profundity when it is known that this liberation leads this same history beyond itself, to a fullness which is beyond the reach of anything that can be foreseen or done by human beings.

While the men who are the objects of the Gospel message are not abstract, a-political beings, but members of a society marked by injustice and the exploitation of some men by others, the Christian community from which the message is proclaimed and which most of these men belong to in one way or another, is not a reality outside history either. Its past and present link it closely to the history of the Latin American people from their early days. Without historical perspective, it is not possible to grasp what is involved in evangelizing nowadays a people to whom the message has been proclaimed already and forms a part of their lives in one way or another. On the other hand, without taking into account the situation of a Church which for the most part is tied to the social order which is being lived in Latin America, no one can grasp what is implied by the liberating character of that evangelization. Those historical and political kinds of conditioning must be analyzed and detailed in order to put into correct focus the proclamation of the message in the Latin American situation.

Solidarity With the Poor

The proclamation of the Gospel from the standpoint of identification with the poor, summons the Church to solidarity with the lower classes of the continent, solidarity with their aspirations and struggles to be present in Latin American history. The Church is called to contribute from its own task, the proclamation of the Gospel, to the abolition of a society built by and for the benefit of a few, and to the construction of a different social order, juster and more human for all.

This process leads to profound breaks and reorientations in the Church of today. They will not, however, be fertile if they express only personal anguish, a crisis of identity, emotional reactions, or impatience, however legitimate all this may be. This road leads only to defensive attitudes, authoritarian measures, gestures inspired by fear or by the search for security, and the endless spiral of conflicts inside the Church. Breaks and reorientations must be radical, must go to the very root of the matter, which in this case extends beyond the narrowly ecclesiastical ambit. The root lies in the way of being a man and a Christian in the present of the Latin American reality; that way consists of identification with the oppressed classes of this continent of injustice and despoilment, which is also a continent of thirst for liberation and hope.

This assumes that there are new experiments in the task of evangelization and convocation into an "ecclesia."[14] There will be different ways of being present in the world of the people, beyond all institutional rigidity. We will have to be prepared to listen to a different voice from the one we are accustomed to hear in the Church. There must be critical awareness of the social and cultural categories which imprison our way of living and proclaiming the Gospel, and make it alien to the world of dominated peoples, marginated races, exploited classes; and even contrary to their profound aspirations towards liberation. It also assumes an authentic search for the Lord in this encounter with the poor, and a lucid explanation of what that spiritual experience signifies.

What is envisaged in this view is the creation of Christian communities in which the private owners of the goods of this world cease to be the masters of the Gospel; communities in which the dispossessed can bring about a social appropriation of the Gospel. Such groups would prophetically proclaim a Church wholly at the service of men in their battle to be men; a creative and critical service always, because rooted in the Gospel. This struggle for manhood follows a way difficult to understand from the old world in which the Word has been and still is lived, thought, and proclaimed. Only by putting down roots among marginated, exploited men and by rising from among these men themselves, from their aspirations, interests, struggles, cultural categories, will a people of

God be forged which will be a Church of the people, which will cause *all* men to listen to the Gospel message and will be a sign of the liberation of the Lord of history.

None of this would have meaning or could even be glimpsed if it were not already outlined, albeit timidly, in trials now going on in various parts of the continent. These attempts start off from the insertion of a growing number of sectors of Christians—workers, professional men, peasants, bishops, students, priests—in the process of liberation in Latin America. Their insertion is official, and is called to greater profundity and to experience, clarification, and purification; it is called to take its place freely and critically within any simplifying political process which fails to take into account all the dimensions of man. It is called to grow, so that the voice of the Christian people of the lower sectors is heard in their own language. There are difficulties in this insertion: the terrain offers hard going at times, with hostility and resistance from those, whether Christians or not, who are tied to the old order of things. But it is a real commitment and is beginning to reveal its fecundity for the liberating option, for an understanding of the faith, and for a proclamation of the Gospel.

The times which are being lived through in Latin America do not allow of any euphoria. The spirituality of the Exodus is no less important than that of the Exile. The joy of the Resurrection requires first death on the Cross—and this can take differing forms. But hope is always there. The situation which is being lived in the continent perhaps makes us live and understand in a renewed form what Paul called "to hope against all hope."

Translated by J. P. Donnelly

DALE VREE

'Christian Marxists': A Critique

A SERIOUS DIALOGUE between Marxists and Christians has been going on in Europe and North America for almost a decade and a half. This dialogue, which has frequently led to theoretical attempts to synthesize Marxism and Christianity, has certainly been intellectually innovative and stimulating. Collaborative political action between Marxists and Christians has been an important political factor in the politics of Italy, France, Spain, Czechoslovakia, and Yugoslavia, but in terms of depth of commitment and readiness to resort to violence, such action has not yet been matched by what can be found in Latin America. There, important segments of the Catholic priesthood and hierarchy have been dramatically radicalized. It is not unusual to see bishops issue statements generally critical of the domestic and inter-American status quo and supportive of socialist and nationalist alternatives. Nor is it unusual to see priests—such as the late, "martyred" Camilo Torres—throw off their cassocks, pick up rifles, and run off with a band of guerrilla warriors. But in terms of political theory, the Latin Americans have been well behind the Europeans and North Americans, who, having felt less urgency to act, have enjoyed more time for scholarship and reflection.

Dale Vree is editor of the "New Oxford Review" and the author of "On Synthesizing Marxism and Christianity." This essay appeared in the May-June 1976 issue of "Freedom at Issue" under the title "Political Transubstantiation" and is reprinted by permission.

A Theology of Liberation (Maryknoll, N.Y.: Orbis Books, 1973), by the Peruvian theologian and activist Gustavo Gutiérrez, is an important attempt to begin to redress the imbalance in theoretical output. Although the thought of Gutiérrez is not as original or complex as that of European dialogue-makers such as Jürgen Moltmann, Ernst Bloch, Johannes Metz, Roger Garaudy, and others, his book is generally recognized as a unique intellectual breakthrough; indeed, as perhaps the most sophisticated voice of Marxist-Christian dialogue in Latin America to date. Contrary to most books of this genre, its significance seems to grow with each passing year. Gutiérrez has emerged as the intellectual spokesman for a new worldwide current in Christian social ethics known as "liberation theology." In the United States, liberation theology has served as the idiom for Christians anxious to promote their favorite liberation movements—particularly black and women's liberation.

More recently, liberation consciousness has been expanding to encompass the entire Third World. In August 1975, the Latin American Secretariat of the U.S. Catholic Conference and the Latin American Working Group of the National Council of Churches sponsored a week-long conference on liberation theology in Detroit—the significance of which was noted and celebrated in *Time* magazine (September 1, 1975) with a full-page story. An appearance by Gustavo Gutiérrez was the main attraction of the conference. Beyond the United States, the World Council of Churches—much like the United Nations—effectively functions as a forum for Third World causes and interests. The World Council has already committed its prestige and its money to the liberation movements directed against the white governments of southern Africa. Indeed, the "pervasive philosophy" of the World Council has become a "'solidarity with the oppressed' liberation theology which recognizes no challengers" (Elliot Wright, "The Good Ship *Oikoumene*," *Worldview*, November 1975, p. 18). Because of the popularity of liberation theology in World Council circles, it would be well to have a closer look at Gutiérrez's *A Theology of Liberation*, the basic guidebook.

Although Gutiérrez borrows frequently from European thinkers, his politico-theological thought is unparalleled by Europeans because he is responding to the Latin American experience. Gutiérrez is not primarily reacting to other people's ideas, but rather to his own existential condition as an inhabitant of the Third World. The difference between the Third World and the developed world is not only geographical; it is also psychological. For the theologian, the situation of the developed world is as Dietrich Bonhoeffer described it: the *mündige Welt* (the world come of age), where technologically competent people no longer feel a need for God. In Latin America, on the other hand, the theologian must respond to quite another situation, a situation where people feel incompetent and helpless, and where suffering is a way of life with no end in sight. Here people *do* feel a need for God, but are at pains to understand how a loving God could have created such an unlovely world.

Inasmuch as the Church is now widely regarded as the most "progressive" institution in Latin America, and insofar as much of Latin America is in a potentially revolutionary situation, we have further reason to examine Gutiérrez's *magnum opus* with some care. It is easy enough to applaud the book as a reflection of the Latin Catholic Church's turning from corruption and concubinage, and toward commitment and change. Be that as it may, "progressive" Latin American Catholic thought (or liberation theology, as it is now called) need no longer be patronized in that way. Liberation theology is ready to stand on its own two feet, to stand up to normal intellectual scrutiny.

Last Things—A Central Theme

A central motif in the international Marxist-Christian dialogue is eschatology, or the doctrine of the Last Things. The theological locution most often associated with eschatology is the "Kingdom of God." Christians have traditionally equated the fullness of the Kingdom of God with the experience of heaven after death. The Kingdom has also been thought to be embryonically present in the heart of the believer as a kind of foretaste of heaven. But rarely has the Kingdom been thought to have any bearing on political matters. However, those Christians who have engaged in dialogue with Marxists have tried to expand the notion of the Kingdom into the hope for an earthly millennial society built—in part at least—by human political action. If this notion of the Kingdom is accepted, and if the full-blown communism of which Marxist-Leninists speak can be understood as a secular version of millennialism, then it is obvious that Christians and Marxists have much in common and every reason to engage in dialogue.

Making eschatology a central motif allows for a much more interesting dialogue than if, say, ethics is made a central motif. A generation ago, such "First World" Christians as Hewlett Johnson (the "Red" Dean of Canterbury) and Harry F. Ward of Union Theological Seminary tended to focus on the ethics of Jesus as the basis for cooperation with Marxists (in particular, with Stalinists). The problem with that approach is twofold: First, Christianity has clearly been more than an ethical system; it has been a *theo*logical system which presumes to talk of God, the mystery of the Kingdom, the meaning of history, and the life of the world to come. To stress ethics is to seem to be too rationalistic and too neglectful of the mystical dimensions of the faith. It is to reduce the Kingdom to an ethical metaphor. Those Christians who get themselves fixated on ethics are too easily suspected of being nothing but ethical humanists—eccentric ones, to be sure. Second, Marxist-Leninists are not really interested in ethics. They are interested in the laws of history and the economy, of which ethics is only an epiphenomenon. A concern with ethics is the hallmark of utopian, not scientific, socialism. Hence, it is very difficult to achieve a sustained intellectual interchange between Christians and Marxists when attention is limited to ethics.

Because of their eschatological focus, present-day Christian dialogue-makers are in a better situation. Yes, they do talk about ethics. But they are really interested in the *dynamics* of historical, economic, and political change—just as the Marxists are. Furthermore, they do not *seem* to be ethical humanists because they are very anxious to talk about God, salvation, providence, prophecy, the Kingdom, and the like—almost all of the paraphernalia of traditional Christianity—in the same breath with which they talk of the dynamics of change. Finally, by going beyond ethics they are better able to sidestep embarrassing questions about the alleged pacifism of Jesus.

This brings us directly to Gustavo Gutiérrez and his *Theology of Liberation*. Without doubt, Gutiérrez is interested in salvation, and his interest in political liberation for Latin America (namely, "liberation" from American hegemony and domestic capitalism) is an integral part of his interest in salvation; indeed, liberation is part of a "single salvific [saving] process" (p. x). This is where matters get intriguing—and sticky. Since the Second Vatican Council, the Catholic Church has been willing to say that political action (or "liberation") has something to do with the Kingdom of God, although it has refused to specify exactly what the relationship is, and has insisted that political goals cannot be identified or equated with the Kingdom.

Were one to say that the Kingdom is political liberation and that liberation is the product of human action, one would all too easily fall into the classical *Pelagian* heresy—that is, one would be saying that man is saved by good works, not grace. To say that is to deny the salvific significance of Christ's atoning sacrifice on the Cross and his Second Coming. It is to deny that God in Christ is the source of salvation. Without Christ, there is no authentic Christianity. Hence it is impossible for a *Christian* to equate liberation with salvation.

But Gutiérrez is unhappy with the recent Catholic position that political action has some (unspecified) relation to the Kingdom. Says he: "It is not enough to say that Christians should not 'shirk' their earthly responsibilities or that these have a 'certain relationship' to salvation" (p. 46).

Although Gutiérrez wants to relate eschatology to politics by uniting liberation and salvation into a single process, he also wants to keep liberation and salvation separate—for fear of sliding into Pelagianism. Traditionally, both Catholics and Protestants have said that salvation—or the Kingdom—is an act, a gift, of God. After all, God saves man; man does not save himself: "For by grace are ye saved through faith, and that not of yourselves, it is the gift of God: not of works, lest any man should boast" (Ephesians 2:8-9).

According to official Catholic theology, the Kingdom "will be the effect solely of divine intervention" (*New Catholic Encyclopedia* [1967], s.v. "Kingdom of God," by M. J. Cantley). The problem for any *theology* of liberation is to talk of salvation as a gift without inducing passivity and indifference to politics—which is frequently what happens. So Gutiérrez's problem is twofold: How can man's political liberation be seen to be a part of a salvific process which finds fulfillment in God's Kingdom—without opening the door to Pelagianism? And how can one talk like a Christian out of one side of one's mouth and like a Pelagian out of the other without choking on the law of non-contradiction?

A Responsibility and a Gift?

Let us hear what Gutiérrez has to say. He sees man "assuming *conscious responsibility* for his own destiny." The result will be "the creation of a new man and a qualitatively different society" (pp. 36-37; italics added). And yet Gutiérrez also says that "the Bible presents liberation—salvation—in Christ as a *total gift* . . ." (p. x; italics added).

But how can the integral "salvific process" be a product of men's "conscious responsibility" as well as a "total gift" from Christ? Is liberation-*cum*-salvation something humans must go out and earn for themselves or not? If so, then it cannot be a "total gift." If not, then it is something humans are not fully responsible for. Gutiérrez does not seem to know whether he wants to be a Christian, a Pelagian, or both. If it is possible to grant that Gutiérrez avoids complete capitulation to Pelagianism, it is not possible to grant that he escapes logical contradiction.

But perhaps what Gutiérrez wants to say is that man must initiate his liberation while God will have to finish it by turning liberation into salvation. This is the most generous interpretation I can come up with. Says Gutiérrez: *"Without liberating historical events, there would be no growth of the Kingdom.* But the process of liberation will not have conquered the very roots of oppression and the exploitation of man by man without the coming Kingdom, which is above all a gift"* (p. 177; italics added). Gutiérrez is trying to protect man's autonomy and free creativity as well as God's sovereignty. But he actually succeeds in both truncating man's autonomy (because man cannot finish what he has started) and compromising God's omnipotence (because God cannot start what he alone can finish). For Gutiérrez, salvation is obviously *contingent* on man's *prior* action. Gutiérrez *wants* to affirm that the coming Kingdom is above all a gift, but one must conclude from what he has said that the coming Kingdom (which he described as the "complete encounter with the Lord," which will "mark an end to history"—p. 168) is first and foremost a product of human action. Enter Pelagius! Enter Thomas Müntzer and a whole host of heretical chiliasts whom Friedrich Engels correctly identified as forerunners of Marxism.

At the root of Gutiérrez's tortuous theologizing is his attempt to blend Marxism with Christianity. By making political liberation a necessary part of the salvific process, Gutiérrez is able to bring Marxism into the drama of Christian salvation. As a result, it is obvious that Marxists are *really* doing God's work. By liberating man, Marxists are freeing God's hands so he can usher in the Kingdom. Hence, Marxists are really Christians incognito.

Gutiérrez says he believes in salvation for everyone—believers and nonbelievers alike. There is no doubt in his mind that God will grant salvation to Marxists, but curiously, there seems to be some doubt that all Christians will be saved. Lest one think Gutiérrez to be a modern ethical humanist, he reminds us that he *does* believe in divine judgment: "We will be definitively judged by our love for men, by our capacity to create brotherly conditions of life" (pp. 198-99). And there is no doubt in Gutiérrez's mind that many, perhaps most, Christians are not measuring up to that standard. So his best pastoral advice to Christians would be to join with Marxists, who are presumed to be actively creating brotherly conditions of life. This is the safest bet—Gutiérrez's version of Pascal's wager! Such counsel sounds bizarre coming from a Catholic priest, but Gutiérrez does not seem to be kidding. Liberation is a precondition for salvation, and, as Gutiérrez repeatedly makes clear, liberation is another term for revolutionary (not social democratic) socialism. And for revolutionary socialism to be efficacious it must be a "scientific" socialism, Gutiérrez tells us. Finally, he leaves no doubt in the reader's mind that he considers Marxian socialism to be scientific (although not necessarily atheistic).

The Spiritual Gifts of Marxists

Not only do the Marxists—unknowingly—hold the keys to the Kingdom of God, but they are undoubtedly spiritually gifted. Since Marxists are very adept at loving mankind, and since loving mankind is the "only way" to have a "true encounter with God" (p. 202), and since "knowledge of God" is actually a "necessary consequence" of loving mankind (p. 206), one is forced to conclude that Marxists are remarkably religious people. Never mind the fact that Marxists do not seem to be aware of their spiritual gifts; Father Gutiérrez is aware of them, and that seems to be what counts. The good Father is empowered to turn bread and wine into Christ's body and blood. Now he presumes to turn Marxists into Christians.

But sometimes I wonder what all this has to do with helping the poor and the powerless. Priests have been notorious for sprinkling holy water on whatever political organization seemed to be the going concern at the time—or the coming concern (in the case of far-sighted priests). Perhaps Marxists should allow themselves to be amused—and tickled—by this sacerdotal sprinkle. Perhaps the water is a good omen for them, signifying that Marxism holds the winning ticket in the race for power in Latin America. (Indeed, Gutiérrez says again and again that he bases his thought on a reading of the "signs of the times" in Latin America.)

But Marxists would do well to bear in mind that the good *padre,* despite his frequent genuflections at the altar of scientific socialism, is no scientific socialist himself. He has *his own—utopian—* reasons for blessing Marxism. For him, "utopian thought" is the basis of scientific knowledge; indeed, it is the source of political action and a "driving force of history" (pp. 232-34). Marxists will perhaps not be surprised that behind this socialist priest there lurks a visionary dreamer. Neither perhaps will more orthodox Catholics (not to mention Protestants and Jews) be surprised that one who places Marxists at the head of God's Elect is nothing but a fanciful utopian.

But let us not forget the prerogatives of priestcraft. In the old pre-Vatican Council days, priests used to stand at the altar with their backs to the people mumbling Latin words through a cloud of incense faster than the speed of sound. "Mumbo-jumbo," the irreverent were wont to call it. Now the priests stand in back of the altar, face the people, and—with the help of microphones—clearly enunciate the words of the Mass in the vernacular of the people. No more mumbo-jumbo. That they save for their books on politics—where Marxists are transformed into Christians by transforming Christians into Marxists.

PART TWO

The Pope's Declaration

There is precious little ambiguity in what John Paul II says about
the Church's *direct* political role: it has none. His address to the
Latin American bishops at Puebla, Mexico, in January 1979 has
been interpreted by some as supporting a politicized Church, but
such interpretations reflect the all-too-human error of finding what
one wants to see instead of what is there.

John Paul II at the start relates his remarks to the 1968 Latin
American Bishops' Conference at Medellín (Colombia), thought
by many to be pivotal in the rise of liberation theology. (Excerpts
from the bishops' Medellín statement appear in Appendixes A and
B of this volume, beginning on page 141, and excerpts from the
bishops' Puebla statement are in Appendixes C-F.) In the introduction to his address he says in effect that any good which flowed
from Medellín should be honored and sustained, and then says he
will not ignore "the incorrect interpretations that have sometimes
resulted and that call for calm discernment, opportune criticism,
and clear-cut stances." Of particular pertinence to the question of
the Church's warrant for political action is this assertion: "Rereadings" of the Gospel can "cause confusion insofar as they
depart from the central criteria of the Church's faith, and people
have the temerity to pass them on as catechesis [church teaching] to
Christian communities." Some people "purport to depict Jesus as a
political activist, as a fighter against Roman domination and the
authorities, and even as someone involved in the class struggle.
This conception of Christ as a political figure, a revolutionary, as
the subversive from Nazareth, does not tally with the Church's
catechesis."

47

Besides making repeated use of the writings of Paul VI, John Paul II also uses his fleeting predecessor to good effect: "In one of his beautiful catechetical instructions, Pope John Paul I alludes to the virtue of hope. Then he says: 'By contrast, it is a mistake to state that political, economic, and social liberation coincide with salvation in Jesus Christ; that the *regnum Dei* [Kingdom of God] is identified with the *regnum hominis* [kingdom of man].' " In such passages the Pope stresses in a powerful way that the Church is not a political actor but *is* a teacher of principle. He argues that the Church "must preach, educate persons and groups, shape public opinion, and give direction to national officials" and that "particular care must be devoted to forming a social conscience at all levels and in all sectors." Such admonitions clearly alert the believer-as-citizen to his duties, and portray the Church as a force in guiding that citizen, but offer no support for a politically activist Church.

JOHN PAUL II

Opening Address at Puebla

**Third General Conference of
Latin American Bishops,
Puebla de Los Angeles, Mexico
January 28, 1979**

BELOVED BROTHERS IN THE EPISCOPATE:

This hour that I have the happiness to experience with
you is certainly a historic one for the Church in Latin America.
World opinion is aware of this; so are the faithful members of your
local churches; and you yourselves, in particular, are aware of it
because you will be the protagonists and responsible leaders of this
hour.

It is also an hour of grace marked by the passing by of the Lord,
by a very special presence and activity of God's Spirit. For this
reason we have confidently invoked this Spirit as we begin our
labors. For this reason also I now want to make the following plea,
speaking to you as a brother to his very beloved brothers: all the
days of this conference and in every one of its proceedings, let

This English translation is from *Evangelization at Present and in the
Future of Latin America*, the Puebla Conclusions (© 1979 by the Na-
tional Conference of Catholic Bishops, 1312 Massachusetts Avenue
N.W., Washington, D.C. 20005).

The following documents are cited by initial letters in this address: EN,
Evangelii Nuntiandi, Paul VI, 1975; GS, *Gaudium et Spes*, Pastoral
Constitution on the Church in the Modern World, Vatican II, 1965; LG,
Lumen Gentium, Dogmatic Constitution on the Church, Vatican II,
1964; MM, *Mater and Magistra*, John XXIII, 1961; OA, *Octogesima
Adveniens*, Paul VI, 1971; PP, *Populorum Progressio*, Paul VI, 1967.

yourselves be led by the Spirit; open up to the Spirit's inspiration and impulse; let it be that Spirit and none other that guides and strengthens you.

Under the guidance of this Spirit, for the third time in the last twenty-five years you are coming together as bishops. You have come here from every country of Latin America, as representatives of the whole Latin American episcopate, to study more deeply as a group the meaning of your mission in the face of the new exigencies of your peoples.

The conference now opening was convoked by our revered Paul VI, confirmed by my unforgettable predecessor, John Paul I, and reconfirmed by me as one of the first acts of my pontificate. It is linked with the already distant conference held in Rio de Janeiro, whose most noteworthy result was the foundation of CELAM.* And it is even more closely linked with your second conference in Medellín, marking its tenth anniversary.

How far humanity has travelled in those ten years! How far the Church has travelled in those ten years in the company and service of humanity! This third conference cannot disregard that fact. So it will have to take Medellín's conclusions as its point of departure, with all the positive elements contained therein, but without disregarding the incorrect interpretations that have sometimes resulted and that call for calm discernment, opportune criticism, and clear-cut stances.

In your debates you will find guidance in the working draft, which was drawn up with great care so that it might serve as a constant point of reference.

But you will also have in your hands Paul VI's Apostolic Exhortation entitled *Evangelii Nuntiandi*. How pleased and delighted that great pontiff was to give his approval to the theme of your conference: "Evangelization in Latin America's Present and Future."

Those close to him during the months when this meeting was being prepared can tell you this. They can also tell you how grateful he was when he learned that the scenario for this whole conference

---

*Consejo Episcopal Latino Americano, the bishops' council.—ED.

would be that text, into which he poured his whole pastoral soul as his life drew to a close. And now that he "has closed his eyes on this world's scene" (Testament of Paul VI), his document becomes a spiritual testament. Your conference will have to scrutinize it lovingly and diligently, making it one of your obligatory touchstones and trying to discover how you can put it into practice. The whole Church owes you a debt of gratitude for what you are doing, for the example you are giving. Perhaps other local churches will take up that example.

The Pope chooses to be with you at the start of your labors, grateful for the gift of being allowed to be with you at yesterday's solemn Mass under the maternal gaze of the Virgin of Guadalupe, and also at this morning's Mass; because "every worthwhile gift, every genuine benefit comes from above, descending from the Father of the heavenly luminaries" (James 1:17). I would very much like to stay with you in prayer, reflection, and work. Be assured that I shall stay with you in spirit while "my anxiety for all the churches" (2 Cor. 11:28) calls me elsewhere. But before I continue my pastoral visit through Mexico and then return to Rome, I want at least to leave you with a few words as a pledge of my spiritual presence. They are uttered with all the concern of a pastor and all the affection of a father. They echo my main preoccupations concerning the theme you are dealing with and the life of the Church in these beloved countries.

I. TEACHERS OF THE TRUTH

It is a great consolation for the universal Pastor to see that you come together here, not as a symposium of experts or a parliament of politicians or a congress of scientists or technologists (however important such meetings may be), but rather as a fraternal gathering of church pastors. As pastors, you keenly realize that your chief duty is to be teachers of the truth: not of a human, rational truth but of the truth that comes from God. That truth includes the principle of authentic human liberation: "You will know the truth, and the truth will set you free" (John 8:32). It is the one and only truth that offers a solid basis for an adequate "praxis."

I,1. Carefully watching over purity of doctrine, basic in building up the Christian community, is therefore the primary and irreplaceable duty of the pastor, of the teacher of faith—in conjunction with the proclamation of the Gospel. How often this was emphasized by St. Paul, who was convinced of the seriousness of carrying out his obligation (1 Tim. 1:3-7; 1:18-20; 1:11-16; 2 Tim. 1:4-14)! Besides oneness in charity, oneness in truth ever remains an urgent demand upon us. In his Apostolic Exhortation *Evangelii Nuntiandi,* our very beloved Paul VI put it this way: "The Gospel that has been entrusted to us is the word of truth. This truth sets us free, and it alone provides peace of heart. It is what people are looking for when we announce the Good News. The truth about God, the truth about human beings and their mysterious destiny, the truth about the world. . . . The preacher of the Gospel will be someone who, even at the cost of renunciation and sacrifice, is always seeking the truth to be transmitted to others. Such a person never betrays or misrepresents the truth out of a desire to please people, to astonish or shock people, to display originality, or to strike a pose. . . . We are pastors of the People of God; our pastoral service bids us to preserve, defend, and communicate the truth, whatever sacrifices may be entailed" (EN 78).

The Truth About Jesus Christ

I,2. From you, pastors, the faithful of your countries expect and demand first and foremost a careful and zealous transmission of the truth about Jesus Christ. This truth is at the core of evangelization and constitutes its essential content: "There is no authentic evangelization so long as one does not announce the name, the teaching, the life, the promises, the Kingdom, the mystery of Jesus of Nazareth, the Son of God" (EN 22).

The vigor of the faith of millions of people will depend on a lively knowledge of this truth. On such knowledge will also depend the strength of their adhesion to the Church and their active presence as Christians in the world. From it will flow options, values, attitudes, and behavior patterns that can give direction and definition to our Christian living, that can create new human beings and then a new humanity through the conversion of the individual and social conscience (EN 18).

It is from a solid Christology that light must be shed on so many of the doctrinal and pastoral themes and questions that you propose to examine in the coming days.

I,3. So we must profess Christ before history and the world, displaying the same deeply felt and deeply lived conviction that Peter did in his profession: "You are the Messiah, . . . the Son of the living God" (Matt. 16:16).

This is the Good News, unique in a real sense. The Church lives by it and for it, even as the Church draws from it all that it has to offer to all human beings, regardless of nation, culture, race, epoch, age, or condition. Hence "on the basis of that profession [Peter's], the history of sacred salvation and of the People of God should take on a new dimension" (John Paul II, Inaugural Homily of His Pontificate, October 22, 1978).

This is the one and only Gospel. And as the apostle wrote so pointedly, "Even if we, or an angel from heaven, should preach to you a gospel not in accord with the one we delivered to you, let a curse be upon him" (Gal. 1:8).

I,4. Now today we find in many places a phenomenon that is not new. We find "rereadings" of the Gospel that are the product of theoretical speculations rather than of authentic meditation on the Word of God and a genuine evangelical commitment. They cause confusion insofar as they depart from the central criteria of the Church's faith, and people have the temerity to pass them on as catechesis to Christian communities.

In some cases people are silent about Christ's divinity, or else they indulge in types of interpretation that are at variance with the Church's faith. Christ is alleged to be only a "prophet," a proclaimer of God's Kingdom and love, but not the true Son of God. Hence, he allegedly is not the center and object of the gospel message itself.

In other cases people purport to depict Jesus as a political activist, as a fighter against Roman domination and the authorities, and even as someone involved in the class struggle. This conception of Christ as a political figure, a revolutionary, as the subversive from Nazareth, does not tally with the Church's catechesis. Confusing the insidious pretext of Jesus' accusers with the attitude of Jesus himself—which was very different—people claim that the cause of his death was the result of a political conflict; they say nothing about the Lord's willing self-surrender or even his awareness of his redemptive mission. The Gospels show clearly that for Jesus anything that would alter his mission as the Servant of Yahweh was a temptation (Matt. 4:8; Luke 4:5). He does not accept the position of those who mixed the things of God with merely political attitudes (Matt. 22:21; Mark 12:17; John 18:36). He unequivocally rejects recourse to violence. He opens his message of conversion to all, and he does not exclude even the publicans. The perspective of his mission goes much deeper. It has to do with complete and integral salvation through a love that brings transformation, peace, pardon, and reconciliation. And there can be no doubt that all this imposes exacting demands on the attitude of any Christians who truly wish to serve the least of their brothers and sisters, the poor, the needy, the marginalized: i.e., all those whose lives reflect the suffering countenance of the Lord (LG 8).

I,5. Against such "rereadings," therefore, and against the perhaps brilliant but fragile and inconsistent hypotheses flowing from them, "evangelization in Latin America's present and future" cannot cease to affirm the Church's faith: Jesus Christ, the Word and Son of God, becomes human to draw close to human beings and to offer them, through the power of his mystery, the great gift of God that is salvation (EN 19,27).

This is the faith that has informed your history, that has shaped what is best in the values of your peoples, and that must continue to animate the dynamics of their future in the most energetic terms. This is the faith that reveals the vocation to concord and unity that must banish the danger of warfare from this continent of hope, a continent in which the Church has been such a potent force for integration. This, in short, is the faith that has found such lively and varied expression among the faithful of Latin America in their religiosity or popular piety.

Rooted in this faith in Christ and in the bosom of the Church, we are capable of serving human beings and our peoples, of penetrating their culture with the Gospel, of transforming hearts, and of humanizing systems and structures.

Any form of silence, disregard, mutilation, or inadequate emphasis on the whole of the mystery of Jesus Christ that diverges from the Church's faith cannot be the valid content of evangelization. "Today, under the pretext of a piety that is false, under the deceptive appearance of a preaching of the gospel message, some people are trying to deny the Lord Jesus," wrote a great bishop in the midst of the hard crises of the fourth century. And he added: "I speak the truth, so that the cause of the confusion that we are suffering may be known to all. I cannot keep silent" (St. Hilary of Poitiers, *Ad Auxentium,* 1-4). Nor can you, the bishops of today, keep silent when his confusion occurs.

This is what Pope Paul VI recommended in his opening address at the Medellín Conference: "Speak, speak, preach, write, take a position, as is said, united in plan and intention, for the defense and elucidation of the truths of the faith, on the relevance of the Gospel, on the questions that interest the life of the faithful and the defense of Christian conduct. . . ."

To fulfill my duty to evangelize all of humanity, I myself will never tire of repeating: "Do not be afraid. Open wide the doors for Christ. To his saving power open the boundaries of State, economic and political systems, the vast fields of culture, civilization, and development" (John Paul II, Inaugural Homily of His Pontificate, October 22, 1978).

The Truth About the Church's Mission

I,6. As teachers of the truth, you are expected to proclaim unceasingly, but with special vigor at this moment, the truth about the mission of the Church, an object of the creed we profess and a basic, indispensable area of our fidelity. The Lord instituted the Church "as a fellowship of life, charity, and truth" (LG 9); as the body, *pleroma,* and sacrament of Christ, in whom dwells the fullness of divinity (LG 7).

The Church is born of our response in faith to Christ. In fact it is by sincere acceptance of the Good News that we believers gather together "in Jesus' name to seek the Kingdom together, build it up, and live it" (EN 13). The Church is the gathering together of "all those who in faith look upon Jesus as the author of salvation and the source of unity and peace" (LG 9).

But on the other hand we are born of the Church. It communicates to us the riches of life and grace entrusted to it. The Church begets us by baptism, nourishes us with the sacraments and the Word of God, prepares us for our mission, and leads us to God's plan—the reason for our existence as Christians. We are the Church's children. With just pride we call the Church our Mother, repeating a title that has come down to us through the centuries from the earliest days (Henri de Lubac, *Méditation sur l'Eglise,* p. 211 ff.).

So we must invoke the Church, respect it, and serve it because "one cannot have God for one's Father if one does not have the Church for one's Mother" (St. Cyprian, *De catholicae ecclesiae unitate,* 6, 8). After all, "how can one possibly love Christ without loving the Church, since the most beautiful testimony to Christ is the following statement of St. Paul: 'He loved the Church and gave himself up for it'?" (EN 16). Or, as St. Augustine puts it: "One possesses the Holy Spirit to the extent that one loves the Church of Christ" (*In Ioannis evangelium,* Tractatus, 32, 8).

Love for the Church must be composed of fidelity and trust. In the first address of my pontificate, I stressed my desire to be faithful to Vatican II, and my resolve to focus my greatest concern on the area of ecclesiology. I invited all to take up once again the Dogmatic Constitution *Lumen Gentium* and "to ponder with renewed earnestness the nature and mission of the Church, its way of existing and operating, . . . not only to achieve that communion of life in Christ among all those who believe and hope in him, but also to help broaden and tighten the oneness of the whole human family" (John Paul II, Message to the Church and the World, October 17, 1978).

Now, at this critical moment in the evangelization of Latin America, I repeat my invitation: "Adherence to this conciliar document, which reflects the light of tradition and contains the dogmatic formulas enunciated a century ago by Vatican I, will provide all of us, both pastors and faithful, a sure pathway and a constant incentive—to say it once again—to tread the byways of life and history" (ibid.).

I,7. Without a well-grounded ecclesiology, we have no guarantee of a serious and vigorous evangelizing activity.

This is so, first of all, because evangelizing is the essential mission, the specific vocation, the innermost identity of the Church, which has been evangelized in turn (EN 14-15; LG 5). Sent out by the Lord, the Church in turn sends out evangelizers to preach "not themselves or their personal ideas, but a Gospel that neither they nor the Church own as their own absolute property, to dispose of as they may see fit . . ." (EN 15). This is so, in the second place, because "for no one is evangelizing an isolated, individual act; rather, it is a profoundly ecclesial action, . . . an action of the Church" (EN 60). Far from being subject to the discretionary authority of individualistic criteria and perspectives, it stands "in communion with the Church and its pastors" (EN 60). Hence a correct vision of the Church is indispensable for a correct view of evangelization.

How could there be any authentic evangelization in the absence of prompt, sincere respect for the sacred magisterium,* a respect based on the clear realization that in submitting to it, the People of God are not accepting the word of human beings but the authentic word of God (1 Thess. 2:13; LG 12)? "The 'objective' importance of this magisterium must be kept in mind and defended against the insidious attacks that now appear here and there against some of the solid truths of our Catholic faith" (John Paul II, Message to the Church and the World, October 17, 1978).

I am well aware of your attachment and availability to the See of Peter and of the love you have always shown it. In the Lord's name I express my heartfelt thanks for the deeply ecclesial outlook implied in that, and I wish you yourselves the consolation of counting on the loyal adherence of your faithful.

---

*The teaching authority of the Church, exercised by the bishops under the headship of the Pope.—ED.

I,8. In the abundant documentation that went into the preparation of this conference, and particularly in the contributions of many Churches, one sometimes notices a certain uneasiness in interpreting the nature and mission of the Church. Allusion is made, for example, to the separation that some set up between the Church and the Kingdom of God. Emptied of its full content, the Kingdom of God is understood in a rather secularist sense: i.e., we do not arrive at the Kingdom through faith and membership in the Church but rather merely by structural change and sociopolitical involvement. Where there is a certain kind of commitment and praxis for justice, there the Kingdom is already present. This view forgets that "the Church . . . receives the mission to proclaim and to establish among all peoples the kingdom of Christ and of God. She becomes on earth the initial budding forth of that kingdom" (LG 5).

In one of his beautiful catechetical instructions, Pope John Paul I alludes to the virtue of hope. Then he says: "By contrast, it is a mistake to state that political, economic, and social liberation coincide with salvation in Jesus Christ; that the *regnum Dei* is identified with the *regnum hominis*" (John Paul I, Catechetical Lesson on the Theological Virtue of Hope, September 20, 1978).

In some instances an attitude of mistrust is fostered toward the "institutional" or "official" Church, which is described as alienating. Over against it is set another, people's Church, one which "is born of the people" and is fleshed out in the poor. These positions could contain varying and not always easily measurable degrees of familiar ideological forms of conditioning. The Council has called our attention to the exact nature and mission of the Church. It has reminded us of the contribution made to its deeper oneness and its ongoing construction by those whose task is to minister to the community and who must count on the collaboration of all the People of God. But let us face the fact: "If the Gospel proclaimed by us seems to be rent by doctrinal disputes, ideological polarizations, or mutual condemnations among Christians, if it is at the mercy of their differing views about Christ and the Church, and even of their differing conceptions of human society and its institutions, . . . how can those to whom we address our preaching fail to be disturbed, disoriented, and even scandalized?" (EN 77).

The Truth About Human Beings

I,9. The truth we owe to human beings is, first and foremost, a truth about themselves. As witnesses to Jesus Christ, we are heralds, spokesmen, and servants of this truth. We cannot reduce it to the principles of some philosophical system, or to mere political activity. We cannot forget it or betray it.

Perhaps one of the most glaring weaknesses of present-day civilization lies in an inadequate view of the human being. Undoubtedly our age is the age that has written and spoken the most about the human being; it is the age of various humanisms, the age of anthropocentrism. But paradoxically it is also the age of people's deepest anxieties about their identity and destiny; it is the age when human beings have been debased to previously unsuspected levels, human values trodden underfoot as never before.

How do we explain this paradox? We can say that it is the inexorable paradox of atheistic humanism. It is the drama of people severed from an essential dimension of their being—the Absolute—and thus confronted with the worst possible diminution of their being. *Gaudium et Spes* goes to the heart of the problem when it says: "Only in the mystery of the incarnate Word does the mystery of man take on light" (GS 22).

Thanks to the Gospel, the Church possesses the truth about the human being. It is found in an anthropology that the Church never ceases to explore more deeply and to share. The primordial assertion of this anthropology is that the human being is the image of God and cannot be reduced to a mere fragment of nature or to an anonymous element in the human city (GS 12, 14). This is the sense intended by St. Irenaeus when he wrote: "The glory of the human being is God; but the receptacle of all God's activity, wisdom, and power is the human being" (St. Irenaeus, *Adversus haereses,* III, 20, 2-3).

I made especially pointed reference to this irreplaceable foundation of the Christian conception of the human being in my Christmas Message: "Christmas is the feast of the human being. . . . Viewed in quantitative terms, the human being is an object of calculation. . . . But at the same time the human being is single, unique, and unrepeatable, someone thought of and chosen from eternity, someone called and identified by name" (John Paul II, Christmas Message, December 25, 1978).

Faced with many other forms of humanism, which frequently are locked into a strictly economic, biological, or psychological view of the human being, the Church has the right and the duty to proclaim the truth about the human being that it received from its teacher, Jesus Christ. God grant that no external coercion will prevent the Church from doing so. But above all, God grant that the Church itself will not fail to do so out of fear or doubt, or because it has let itself be contaminated by other brands of humanism, or for lack of confidence in its original message.

So when a pastor of the Church clearly and unambiguously announces the truth about the human being, which was revealed by him who knew "what was in man's heart" (John 2:25), he should be encouraged by the certainty that he is rendering the best service to human beings.

This complete truth about human beings is the basis of the Church's social teaching, even as it is the basis of authentic liberation. In the light of this truth we see that human beings are not the pawns of economic or political processes, that instead these processes are geared toward human beings and subject to them.

I have no doubt that this truth about human beings, as taught by the Church, will emerge strengthened from this pastoral meeting.

II. SIGNS AND BUILDERS OF UNITY

Your pastoral service to the truth is complemented by a like service to unity.

Unity Among the Bishops

II,1. First of all, it will be a unity among you yourselves, the bishops. As one bishop, St. Cyprian, put it in an era when communion among the bishops of his country was greatly threatened: "We must guard and maintain this unity . . . we bishops, in particular, who preside over the Church, so that we may bear witness to the fact that the episcopate is one and indivisible. Let no one mislead the faithful or alter the truth. The episcopate is one . . ." (St. Cyprian, *De catholicae ecclesiae unitate,* 6, 8).

This episcopal unity does not come from human calculation or maneuvering, but from on high: from service to one single Lord, from the inspiration of one single Spirit, from love for one and the same unique Church. It is the unity resulting from the mission that Christ has entrusted to us. Here on the Latin American continent that mission has been going on for almost half a millennium. Today you are boldly carrying it on in an age of profound transformations, as we approach the close of the second millennium of redemption and ecclesial activity. It is unity centered around the Gospel of the body and blood of the Lamb, of Peter living in his successors; all of these are different but important signs of Jesus' presence in our midst.

What an obligation you have, dear brothers, to live this pastoral unity at this conference! The conference itself is a sign and fruit of the unity that already exists; but it is also a foretaste and anticipation of what should be an even more intimate and solid unity! So begin your labors in an atmosphere of fraternal unity. Even now let this unity be a component of evangelization.

Unity With Priests, Religious, and the Faithful

II,2. Unity among the bishops finds its extension in unity with priests, religious,* and the faithful laity. Priests are the immediate collaborators of the bishops in their pastoral mission. This mission would be compromised if close unity did not exist between priests and their bishops.

Men and women religious are also particularly important subjects of that unity. I know well how important their contribution to evangelization has been, and continues to be, in Latin America. They arrived here in the dawning light of discovery, and they were here when almost all your countries were taking their first steps. They have labored here continually by the side of the diocesan clergy. In some countries more than half of your priests are religious; in others the vast majority are. This alone indicates how important it is here, even more than in other parts of the world, for

---

*Members of a religious order living in community, under a common rule, observing vows of poverty, chastity, and obedience, and dedicated to the service of God.—ED.

religious to not only accept but loyally strive for an indissoluble unity of outlook and action with their bishops. To the bishops the Lord entrusted the mission of feeding the flock. To religious belongs the task of blazing the trail for evangelization. Bishops cannot and should not fail to have the collaboration of religious, whose charism makes them all the more available as agents in the service of the Gospel. And their collaboration must be not only active and responsible, but also docile and trusting. In this connection a heavy obligation weighs on everyone in the ecclesial community to avoid parallel magisteria, which are ecclesially unacceptable and pastorally sterile.

Lay people are also subjects of this unity, whether involved as individuals or joined in organs of the apostolate for the spread of God's Kingdom. It is they who must consecrate the world to Christ in the midst of their day-to-day tasks and in their varied family and professional functions, maintaining close union with, and obedience to, their legitimate pastors.

This precious gift of ecclesial unity must be safeguarded among all those who are part of the wayfaring People of God, in line with what *Lumen Gentium* said.

III.   DEFENDERS AND PROMOTERS OF HUMAN DIGNITY

III,1. Those familiar with the history of the Church know that in every age there have been admirable bishops deeply involved in the valiant defense of the human dignity of those entrusted to them by the Lord. Their activity was always mandated by their episcopal mission, because they regarded human dignity as a gospel value that cannot be despised without greatly offending the Creator.

On the level of the individual, this dignity is crushed underfoot when due regard is not maintained for such values as freedom, the right to profess one's religion, physical and psychic integrity, the right of life's necessities, and the right to life itself. On the social and political level it is crushed when human beings cannot exercise their right to participate, when they are subjected to unjust and illegitimate forms of coercion, when they are subjected to physical and psychic torture, and so forth.

I am not unaware of the many problems in this area that are being faced in Latin America today. As bishops, you cannot fail to concern yourselves with them. I know that you propose to reflect seriously on the relationships and implications existing between evangelization and human promotion or liberation, focusing on the specific nature of the Church's presence in this broad and important area.

Here is where we come to the concrete, practical application of the themes we have touched upon in talking about the truth about Christ, about the Church, and about the human being.

III,2. If the Church gets involved in defending or promoting human dignity, it does so in accordance with its mission. For even though that mission is religious in character, and not social or political, it cannot help but consider human persons in terms of their whole being. In the parable of the Good Samaritan, the Lord outlined the model way of attending to all human needs (Luke 10:30 ff.); and he said that in the last analysis he will identify himself with the disinherited—the imprisoned, the hungry, and the abandoned—to whom we have offered a helping hand (Matt. 25:31 ff.). In these and other passages of the Gospel (Mark 6:35-44), the Church has learned that an indispensable part of its evangelizing mission is made up of works on behalf of justice and human promotion (see the Final Document of the Synod of Bishops, October 1971). It has learned that evangelization and human promotion are linked together by very strong ties of an anthropological, theological, and charitable nature (EN 31). Thus "evangelization would not be complete if it did not take into account the mutual interaction that takes hold in the course of time between the Gospel and the concrete personal and social life of the human being" (EN 29).

Let us also keep in mind that the Church's activity in such areas as human promotion, development, justice, and human rights is always intended to be in the service of the human being, the human being as seen by the Church in the Christian framework of the anthropology it adopts. The Church therefore does not need to have recourse to ideological systems in order to love, defend, and collaborate in the liberation of the human being. At the center of the message of which the Church is the trustee and herald, it finds inspiration for acting in favor of brotherhood, justice, and peace, and against all forms of domination, slavery, discrimination, violence, attacks on religious liberty, and aggression against human beings and whatever attacks life (GS 26, 27, 29).

III,3. It is therefore not out of opportunism or a thirst for novelty that the Church, the "expert in humanity" (Paul VI, Address to the United Nations, October 5, 1965), defends human rights. It is prompted by an authentically evangelical commitment which, like that of Christ, is primarily a commitment to those most in need.

In fidelity to this commitment, the Church wishes to maintain its freedom with regard to the opposing systems, in order to opt solely for the human being. Whatever the miseries or sufferings that afflict human beings, it is not through violence, power-plays, or political systems but through the truth about human beings that they will find their way to a better future.

III,4. From this arises the Church's constant preoccupation with the delicate question of property ownership. One proof of this is to be found in the writings of the Church Fathers during the first thousand years of Christianity's existence (St. Ambrose, *de Nabuthae*, c. 12, n. 53). It is demonstrated by the vigorous and oft reiterated teaching of St. Thomas Aquinas. In our day the Church has appealed to the same principles in such far-reaching documents as the social encyclicals of the recent popes. Pope Paul VI spoke out on this matter with particular force and profundity in his encyclical *Populorum Progressio* (PP 23-24; MM 104-15)

This voice of the Church, echoing the voice of the human conscience, did not cease to make itself heard down through the centuries, amid the most varied sociocultural systems and circumstances. It deserves and needs to be heard in our age as well, when the growing affluence of a few people parallels the growing poverty of the masses.

It is then that the Church's teaching, which says that there is a *social mortgage* on all private property, takes on an urgent character. Insofar as this teaching is concerned, the Church has a mission to fulfill. It must preach, educate persons and groups, shape public opinion, and give direction to national officials. In so doing, it will be working for the good of society. Eventually this Christian, evangelical principle will lead to a more just and equitable distribution of goods, not only within each nation but also in the wide world as a whole. And this will prevent the stronger countries from using their power to the detriment of the weaker ones.

Those in charge of the public life of states and nations will have to realize that internal and international peace will be assured only when a social and economic system based on justice takes effect.

Christ did not remain indifferent in the face of this vast and demanding imperative of social morality. Neither could the Church. In the spirit of the Church, which is the spirit of Christ, and supported by its ample, solid teaching, let us get back to work in this field.

Here I must once again emphasize that the Church's concern is for the whole human being.

Thus an indispensable condition for a just economic system is that it foster the growth and spread of public education and culture. The juster an economy is, the deeper will be its cultural awareness. This is very much in line with the view of Vatican II: i.e., that to achieve a life worthy of a human being, one cannot limit oneself to *having more;* one must strive to *be more* (GS 35).

So drink at these authentic fonts, brothers. Speak in the idiom of Vatican II, John XXIII, and Paul VI. For that is the idiom that embodies the experience, the suffering, and the hope of contemporary humanity.

When Paul VI declared that development is the new name for peace (PP 76-79), he was thinking of all the ties of interdependence existing, not only within nations, but also between them on a worldwide scale. He took into consideration the mechanisms that are imbued with materialism rather than authentic humanism, and that therefore lead on the international level to the ever increasing wealth of the rich at the expense of the ever increasing poverty of the poor.

There is no economic norm that can change those mechanisms in and by itself. In international life, too, one must appeal to the principles of ethics, the exigencies of justice, and the primary commandment of love. Primacy must be given to that which is moral, to that which is spiritual, to that which flows from the full truth about the human being.

I wanted to voice these reflections to you, since I regard them as very important; but they should not distract you from the central theme of this conference. We will reach human beings, we will reach justice through evangelization.

III,5. In the light of what has been said above, the Church is profoundly grieved to see "the sometimes massive increase in violations of human rights in many parts of the world. . . . Who can deny that today there are individual persons and civil authorities who are violating fundamental rights of the human person with impunity? I refer to such rights as the right to be born; the right to life; the right to responsible procreation; the right to work; the right to peace, freedom, and social justice; and the right to participate in making decisions that affect peoples and nations. And what are we to say when we run up against various forms of collective violence, such as racial discrimination against individuals and groups and the physical and psychological torturing of prisoners and political dissidents? The list grows when we add examples of abduction and of kidnapping for the sake of material gain, which represent such a traumatic attack on family life and the social fabric" (John Paul II, Message to the United Nations, December 2, 1978). We cry out once more: Respect the human being, who is the image of God! Evangelize so that this may become a reality, so that the Lord may transform hearts and humanize political and economic systems, with the responsible commitment of human beings as the starting point!

III,6. Pastoral commitments in this field must be nurtured with a correct Christian conception of liberation. "The Church . . . has the duty of proclaiming the liberation of millions of human beings, . . . the duty of helping to bring about this liberation" (EN 30). But it also has the corresponding duty of proclaiming liberation in its deeper, fuller sense, the sense proclaimed and realized by Jesus (EN 31 ff.). That fuller liberation is "liberation from everything that oppresses human beings, but especially liberation from sin and the evil one, in the joy of knowing God and being known by him" (EN 9). It is liberation made up of reconciliation and forgiveness. It is liberation rooted in the fact of being the children of God, whom we are now able to call Abba, Father! (Rom. 8:15). It is liberation that enables us to recognize all human beings as our brothers or sisters, as people whose hearts can be transformed by God's mercifulness. It is liberation that pushes us, with all the force of love, toward communion; and we find the fullness and culmination of that communion in the Lord. It is liberation as the successful conquest of the forms of bondage and idols fashioned by human beings, as the growth and flowering of the new human being.

It is a liberation that, in the framework of the Church's specific mission, "cannot be reduced simply to the restricted domain of economics, politics, society, or culture, . . . can never be sacrificed to the requirements of some particular strategy, some short-term praxis or gain" (EN 33).

If we are to safeguard the originality of Christian liberation and the energies that it is capable of releasing, we must at all costs avoid reductionism and ambiguity. As Paul VI pointed out: "The Church would lose its innermost meaning. Its message of liberation would have nothing original, and it would lend itself to ready manipulation and expropriation by ideological systems and political parties" (EN 32). There are many signs that help us to distinguish when the liberation in question is Christian and when, on the other hand, it is based on ideologies that make it inconsistent with an evangelical view of humanity, of things, and of events (EN 35). These signs derive from the content that the evangelizers proclaim or from the concrete attitudes that they adopt. At the level of content one must consider how faithful they are to the Word of God, to the Church's living tradition, and to its magisterium. As for attitudes, one must consider what sense of communion they feel, with the bishops first of all, and then with the other sectors of God's People. Here one must also consider what contribution they make to the real building up of the community; how they channel their love into caring for the poor, the sick, the dispossessed, the neglected, and the oppressed; and how, discovering in these people the image of the poor and suffering Jesus, they strive to alleviate their needs and to serve Christ in them (LG 8). Let us make no mistake about it: as if by some evangelical instinct, the humble and simple faithful spontaneously sense when the Gospel is being served in the Church and when it is being eviscerated and asphyxiated by other interests.

As you see, the whole set of observations on the theme of liberation that were made by *Evangelii Nuntiandi* retain their full validity.

III,7. All that we have recalled above constitutes a rich and complex heritage, which *Evangelii Nuntiandi* calls the social doctrine, or social teaching, of the Church (EN 38). This teaching comes into being, in the light of God's Word and the authentic magisterium, from the presence of Christians in the midst of the world's changing situations and their contact with the resultant challenges. So this social doctrine entails not only principles for reflection but also norms for judgment and guidelines for action (OA 4).

To place responsible confidence in this social doctrine, even though some people try to sow doubts and lack of confidence in it; to study it seriously; to try to apply it; to teach it and to be loyal to it: in children of the Church, all this guarantees the authenticity of their involvement in delicate and demanding social tasks, and of their efforts on behalf of the liberation or advancement of their fellow human beings.

Permit me, then, to commend to your special pastoral attention the urgency of making your faithful aware of the Church's social doctrine.

Particular care must be devoted to forming a social conscience at all levels and in all sectors. When injustices increase and the gap between rich and poor widens distressingly, then the social doctrine of the Church—in a form that is creative and open to the broad areas of the Church's presence—should be a valuable tool for formation and action. This holds true for the laity in particular:

"Secular duties and activities belong properly, although not exclusively, to laymen" (GS 43). It is necessary to avoid supplanting the laity, and to study seriously just when certain ways of substituting for them retain their *raison d'être*. Is it not the laity who are called, by virtue of their vocation in the Church, to make their contribution in the political and economic areas, and to be effectively present in the safeguarding and advancing of human rights?

IV. SOME PRIORITY TASKS

You are going to consider many pastoral topics of great importance. Time prevents me from mentioning them. I have referred to some, or will do so, in my meetings with priests, religious, seminarians, and lay people.

For various reasons, the topics I mention here are of great importance. You will not fail to consider them, among the many others your pastoral perspicacity will indicate to you.

a. The family: Make every effort to ensure that there is pastoral care for the family. Attend to this area of such priority importance, certain that evangelization in the future depends largely on the "domestic Church." The family is the school of love, of knowledge of God, of respect for life and human dignity. This pastoral field is all the more important because the family is the object of so many threats. Think of the campaigns advocating divorce, the use of contraceptives, and abortion, which destroy society.

b. Priestly and religious vocations: Despite an encouraging revival of vocations, the lack of vocations is a grave and chronic problem in most of your countries. There is an immense disproportion between the growing number of inhabitants and the number of workers engaged in evangelization. This is of immeasurable importance to the Christian community. Every community must acquire its vocations, just as a proof of its vitality and maturity. An intensive pastoral effort must be reactivated. Starting off from the Christian vocation in general and an enthusiastic pastoral effort among young people, such an effort will give the Church the servants it needs. Lay vocations, indispensable as they are, cannot be a satisfactory compensation. What is more, one of the proofs of the laity's commitment is the abundance of vocations to the consecrated life.

c. Young people: How much hope the Church places in them! How much energy needed by the Church circulates through young people in Latin America! How close we pastors must be to young people, so that Christ and the Church and brotherly love may penetrate deeply into their hearts!

V. CONCLUSION

Closing this message, I cannot fail to call down once again the protection of the Mother of God upon your persons and your work during these days. The fact that this meeting of ours is taking place in the spiritual presence of Our Lady of Guadalupe—who is venerated in Mexico and in all other countries as the mother of the Church in Latin America—is a cause of joy and a source of hope for me. May she, the "star of evangelization," be your guide in the reflections you make and the decisions you arrive at. From her divine Son may she obtain for you:

— the boldness of prophets and the evangelical prudence of pastors;
— the clearsightedness of teachers and the confident certainty of guides and directors;
— courage as witnesses, and the calmness, patience, and gentleness of fathers.

May the Lord bless your labors. You are accompanied by select representatives: priests, deacons, men and women religious, lay people, experts, and observers. Their collaboration will be very useful to you. The eyes of the whole Church are on you, in confidence and hope. You intend to measure up to their expectations, in full fidelity to Christ, the Church, and humanity. The future is in God's hands. But somehow God is also placing the future of a new evangelization impetus in your hands: "Go, therefore, and make disciples of all nations" (Matt. 28:19).

PART THREE

Interpreting Puebla

Michael Novak's essay examines the critical impact of the Pope's Puebla address on the pretensions of liberation theology. Puebla, he says, rejects and repudiates much of the presumption under which religion is made to serve political ends in the doctrines of liberation theology. Novak makes it clear why the practitioners and preachers of liberation theology would want to ignore Puebla or, if more convenient, redefine it so as to neutralize its impact on Catholic thinking.

In the second essay, Father James Schall shows how the American press distorted the meaning of the Puebla address. The simple expedients of "contextualizing" and "relativizing" the reading of the text—"Do not read these simple words without the aid of Expert Interpreters"—are enough to bathe even the simplest observations in fog. How convenient for the Experts to say a *plain* reading is not enough, so that the Pope, thought to be a teacher to all Catholics, in fact becomes a teacher only to Experts, who *then* teach the flock. John Paul II hardly needs such help.

Both Novak and Schall believe the Pope's address reflects the mainstream of Catholic thinking. They find, as the Pope does, that the Gospel points to human values and ends but not to specific political means. They find John Paul II fully aware that any economic system must aim at the common welfare and must not be built on human exploitation. But human *sufficiency,* not human *sameness,* is the true economic objective. Sufficiency in human terms demands abundance. And so a Gospel-based economic system would need incentive, drive, and human dynamism adequate to achieve economic abundance. And it would want, to the extent possible, to secure these without denying personal choice.

Thus Novak and Schall see in Puebla what has been present in all mainstream Catholic economic teaching of the modern era: if the Gospel is our guide, presumably we want an economic system aimed at sufficiency and personal initiative and latitude, and also designed to offset the human suffering inherent in any system that must sometimes allocate scarcity.

Balance, synthesis, reconciliation of values rather than the monolithic pursuit of any single value—this has been the economic teaching of the modern Catholic Church. And its companion is that the political order, not the Church, finally establishes, measures, and alters the economic means by which that balance is to be achieved.

MICHAEL NOVAK

Liberation Theology and the Pope

ON HIS HIGHLY PUBLICIZED voyage to Mexico late in January 1979, Karol Wojtyla, only recently become Pope John Paul II, faced two systems of authoritarianism. He faced Latin American feudal regimes of a cruelty well known to the bishops he was about to address, some of whom had experienced prison themselves. And he faced a rising enthusiasm, particularly on the part of foreign-trained Latin American clergymen, for "Marxist liberation."

The Pope addressed the Conference of Latin American Bishops (CELAM) at Puebla on January 28. At first his 8,000-word sermon drew words of disappointment and sarcasm from many of the "liberation theologians" he was taken to be attacking. Then began a process by which the Pope's straight sentences were gradually softened and transmuted until, we were told by the *New York Times* (February 18), the theologians in question celebrated the end of the conference by drinking beer, singing "folk songs from all

Michael Novak is a resident scholar in religion and public policy at the American Enterprise Institute in Washington, D.C. He formerly taught at Stanford and at Syracuse University. His most recent book is "The Spirit of Democratic Capitalism." This essay originally appeared in "Commentary" magazine, June 1979 (reprinted by permission; all rights reserved). The translation of the Pope's Puebla address that Mr. Novak quotes differs slightly from the translation printed in full in this book.

73

over the continent," so that "well past midnight their songs echoed through the streets . . . sounding suspiciously like a victory celebration." What had actually happened? Had the Pope attacked "liberation theology" or had he given it official sanction?

The meeting at Puebla was the third major meeting of CELAM in twenty-five years. At the first one in Rio de Janeiro, the bishops of Latin America had established a continent-wide organization. Over the years, they formulated some fairly clear views about their own special needs and the general need for a reorganization of the international church. Thus, at the Second Vatican Council (1961-65), their regional unity was already conspicuous, and their interventions helped the "progressive" forces at the Council do much more than expected. Then in 1968—the year of vast student unrest in the United States, Mexico, France, and elsewhere—the bishops met for the second time, at Medellín, Colombia, and produced a document that addressed the public-policy needs of the continent. Tinged with Marxist rhetoric, that document gave rise, two years later, to the first writings self-described as "liberation theology," that is, formal attempts to translate Christianity into Marxist categories. Works in this genre have multiplied since.

Pope John Paul II went straight to the heart of all this in the opening paragraphs of his address at Puebla. He said immediately that his "point of departure" was "the conclusions of Medellín" as well as the sympathetic support of those conclusions by Pope Paul VI in *Evangelii Nuntiandi*. But he did not hesitate to qualify his praise of "all the positive elements" that the Medellín conclusions contained, with the warning that he was not about to ignore the "incorrect interpretations at times made and which call for calm discernment, opportune criticism, and clear choices of position."

The misconception, the confusion which the Pope wished to sweep away was that Christianity is reducible to Marxist categories. He opposed those "rereadings" of the Gospel that "cause confusion by diverging from the central criteria of the faith of the Church." He opposed those for whom "the Kingdom of God is emptied of its full content and is understood in a rather secularist sense," as if it were to be reached "by mere changing of structures and social and political involvement, and as being present wherever there is a certain type of involvement and activity for justice."

And he particularly opposed those who "claim to show Jesus as politically committed, as one who fought against Roman oppression and the authorities, and also as one involved in the class struggle. This idea of Christ as a political figure, a revolutionary, as the subversive man from Nazareth, does not tally with the Church's catechesis."

The Pope observed that "our age is the one in which man has been most written and spoken of," yet it is also "the age of man's abasement to previously unsuspected levels, the age of human values trampled on as never before." Like Solzhenitsyn in his commencement address at Harvard in 1978, Pope John Paul II attributed this to "the inexorable paradox of atheistic humanism." By contrast, "the primordial affirmation of [Catholic] anthropology is that man is God's image and cannot be reduced to a mere portion of nature or a nameless element in the human city." He rejected a "strictly economic, biological, or psychological view of man," insisting instead that "the complete truth about the human being constitutes the foundation of the Church's social teaching and the basis of true liberation. In the light of this truth, man is not a being subjected to economic or political processes; these processes are instead directed to man and subjected to him." It is necessary, in short, to reject a materialistic interpretation of history and to defend the primacy of the spiritual.

At this point, Pope John Paul II showed himself in consonance with the traditional political philosophies of Western civilization. Tocqueville, for example, had made a similar observation: "There is no religion which does not place the object of man's desire above and beyond the treasures of the earth, and which does not naturally raise his soul to regions far above those of the senses. Nor is there any which does not impose on man some sort of duties to his mind, and thus draws him at times from the contemplation of himself." Correspondingly, the Pope discerned in "human dignity a gospel value that cannot be despised without greatly offending the Creator," and then launched one of his two explicit condemnations of Latin American practices:

> This dignity is infringed on the individual level when due regard is not had for values such as freedom, the right to essential goods, to life. . . . It is infringed on the social and political level when

man cannot exercise his right of participation, or when he is subjected to unjust and unlawful coercion, or submitted to physical or mental torture, etc. I am not unaware of how many questions are being posed in this sphere today in Latin America.

The Pope then turned to problems of action. The mission of the Church, he said, "although it is religious and not social or political, cannot fail to consider man in the entirety of his being." This mission "has as an essential part action for justice and the tasks of the advancement of man." But the Church "does not need to have recourse to ideological systems in order to love, defend, and collaborate in the liberation of man . . . acting in favor of brotherhood, justice, and peace, and against all foes of domination, slavery, discrimination, violence, attacks on religious liberty, and aggression against man, and whatever attacks life." The Church has a commitment, like Christ's, "to the most needy. In fidelity to this commitment, the Church wishes to stay free with regard to the competing systems, in order to opt only for man."

The Pope then went on to define liberation in a Christian way, first positively, and then with this negative: "Liberation . . . in the framework of the Church's proper mission is not reduced to the simple and narrow economic, political, social, or cultural dimension, and is not sacrificed to the demands of any strategy, practice, or short-term solution." The important thing is "to safeguard the originality of Christian liberation," and "to avoid any form of curtailment or ambiguity" which would cause the Church to "lose her fundamental meaning" and leave her open to "manipulation by ideological systems and political parties."

The Liberation Center

What is the liberation theology to which the Pope so clearly addressed himself? The headquarters for liberation theology in the United States, and perhaps in the entire world, are located near the Hudson River at Maryknoll, New York, international center of America's most active missionary order, the Maryknoll Fathers and Sisters. In a bibliography of Third World theologies, 32 of 82 titles were published by Maryknoll's Orbis Books. Founded in 1970, Orbis announced that it "draws its imperatives from and orders its priorities on the fact that the majority of Christians live in the affluent countries of the North Atlantic community, which controls almost 80 per cent of the world's resources but accounts for only 20 per cent of the world's population. . . . Christians bear a heavy responsibility for a world that can annually 'afford' to spend $150 billion on arms, but can scarcely scrape together $10 billion for economic and social development." At the heart of the matter, according to the initial Orbis release, was the need for a change in intellectual focus: "Total development will demand the restructuring of oppressive political and social orders wherever they exist, in Calcutta or Chicago, New York or Recife. For this reason, the word *development* should be replaced by *liberation.*"

It is quite remarkable that the list of cities requiring liberation did not include Cracow or Leningrad, Havana or Peking, Hanoi or Prague. The complete Orbis catalogue of 141 titles, as of the end of 1978, maintains this distinction intact. Thirty-nine titles are concentrated on Latin America, a few on Africa and other places, none on Communist lands.

The focus on Latin America is not accidental. Liberation theology is mainly, although not entirely, a product of the Spanish-speaking world. Father Sergio Torres of Chile, lecturer at Maryknoll, describes his world view and that of his fellow Latin American theologians in this way:

> What we understand is that we are at the end of a stage in the history of the world. Europe and Western society is no longer making the history of the world as it has been since the Roman empire. We understand that history is now being made by the peoples of the Third World. The oil crisis is getting that through here in the United States. . . . We in Latin America are the only continent that is both Christian and underdeveloped, so we are in a special place. We will start a new understanding of the faith because we belong to the churches, Catholic and Protestant, and are living in a situation which makes them functional to the systems. . . . The process of colonization, liberation, and organization is best understood in Marxist terms.

Father Miguel D'Escoto, a Nicaraguan, the director of communications at Maryknoll, adds:

> As Latin Americans, we know capitalism in a way young people here don't know it. We had no New Deal, no Roosevelt to come along and soften it up. Capitalism is intrinsically wrong at its base. The basic concept is that man is selfish, and being realistic, we should accept this and cater to it rather than change it.

The chief systematizer of liberation theology, Father Juan Luis Segundo, whose five-volume treatise *Theology for Artisans of a New Humanity* has sold 64,000 copies, told a group of American Jesuits:

> There is no perfect solution. The only way is for us to choose between two oppressions. And the history of Marxism, even oppressive, offers right now more hope than the history of existing capitalism. . . . Marx did not create the class struggle, international capitalism did.

The most widely read of all the liberation theologians is Father Gustavo Gutiérrez of Peru, whose *A Theology of Liberation* (Orbis) has sold 45,000 copies. He writes:

> It is undeniable that the class struggle plants problems for the universality of Christian love and church unity. But every consideration on this matter ought to begin with two elemental attestations: class struggle is a fact and neutrality in this matter is impossible.

But it is not merely the theologians and the priests of Latin America who have looked upon Marxism with favor. Distinguished bishops, like the Bishop of Cuernavaca, Arceo Mendez, and the Archbishop of Recife, Dom Helder Camara, have been unambiguous in their preference for Marxism. Archbishop Camara, for example, addressed the University of Chicago's celebration of the Seventh Centenary of St. Thomas Aquinas in these terms:

> When a man, whether philosopher or not, attracts irresistibly millions of human beings, especially young people; when a man becomes the inspiration for life and for death of a great part of humanity, and makes the powerful of the earth tremble with hate and fear, this man deserves to be studied. . . . As the University of Chicago chose to take upon herself the responsibility

of celebrating St. Thomas Aquinas's Seventh Centenary, we have the right to suggest that the best way to honor the centenary . . . should be for the University of Chicago to try to do with Karl Marx what St. Thomas, in his day, did with Aristotle.

The social and intellectual background of the liberation theologians is germane to their views. When I was studying theology in Rome at the Gregorian University in 1956-58, I became familiar with some of the Latin American and Spanish seminarians, and several clear impressions about their political-theological culture fixed themselves in my mind. First, it was obvious that they chafed under the image of Latin cultures which prevailed in the English-speaking world. They were, they felt, the victims of an Anglo-Saxon ethnocentric bias, a Protestant bias to boot, and a bias informed by the sort of individualism, pragmatism, and materialism they found especially abhorrent. Some seemed, in effect, to be still carrying in mind the long-ago defeat of the Spanish Armada in much the same way some Southerners recall the humiliation of defeat in the Civil War.

Many of these bright young men studied not only in Rome but in Belgium and France and Germany as well. There they shared in what was then known as *nouvelle théologie*—that contemporary reaction against Thomism, strong on scriptural studies and "salvation history," intensely preoccupied with the renewal of the Church from biblical and patristic sources (and hostile to the theory of Christian democracy developed by Thomists like Jacques Maritain). On their return to Latin America, many of them became involved in the movements organizing peasants in credit unions and agrarian cooperatives. Much of their earlier training seemed far too theological, and they reacted with a veritably Oedipal vehemence against their European teachers.

Yet in their work among the peasants, many found themselves already upstaged by Marxist organizers; as for the sophisticated French and German theology they brought to the peasants, it served little useful purpose. So the younger clergy began to attend more intently to the indigenous piety of the people. They discovered the power of popular religion. In its quiet endurance and strength, they found new theological resources—resources, moreover, which served to differentiate them from the despised Yankee experts and technicians who imported into Latin America the strange and threatening concepts of "development" capitalist-style. In expressing their resentment of the Northern experts, such activists have had no better spokesman than the brilliant but erratic Ivan Illich of Cuernavaca, whose anti-institutional reflections have become so popular in radical circles in North America.

The Latin American Context

When the Latin American liberation theologians speak of "class struggle," they are thinking primarily of the struggle within feudalism of landholders and peasants, hardly at all of the classic Marxist picture of an industrial proletariat. (What Latin Americans persist in calling "capitalism" is, in Latin America, largely a form of syndicalism or corporatism, which descends from the rights given by the Spanish or Portuguese crown to certain large landholders or adventurers and constitutes virtual monopoly or state mercantilism.) Both the Industrial Revolution and the social revolution that would have broken the power of the traditional landholders, as the Glorious Revolution did in Great Britain, have hardly been known among them. In most of Latin America, the middle class is quite small, and "bourgeois values," of the sort well established in the North Atlantic world, scarcely exist.

The full effect of the Protestant spirit of dissent and individual conscience has thus not been felt in Latin cultures. By the same token, the compensating social forces of pragmatic compromise, voluntary association, and cooperative fellow-feeling that characterize Anglo-American individualism are equally missing in Latin American politics. Latin forms of idealism and romanticism make for acute political fractionalization. There is in Latin America little scope for the entrepreneur, for invention, for enterprise. There are few Horatio Algers. The virtues most celebrated—honor, nobility, dignity—are the opposite of bourgeois.

The system confronted by Latin American Catholics is one of entrenched inequality, in which powerful landholders (often of early Spanish stock) have power and privileges far removed from those of peasants and workers (often of Indian stock). The Latin American elites lack those traditions of service, stewardship, and public-spiritedness that within the United States have softened the impact of economic elites upon political life. The lower classes in Latin America have had little opportunity to develop the political consciousness which has characterized the Anglo-Saxon yeoman for several centuries, and have scarcely shared in the traditions of "the rights of Englishmen" which have affected Anglo-Saxon consciousness.

The picture is further clouded by the powerful traditions of a strong, authoritarian military. In many Latin American countries, a military career has offered ambitious youngsters more opportunities for higher education and advancement than any other profession. Not infrequently, the military provides leaders of idealistic tendencies both on the socialist and on the democratic side. In recent years, however, military regimes have grown more "modern" in precisely the least humane ways: in the techniques of cruel repression.

All this, moreover, takes place in an environment in which European ideologies—both the Fascism of the World War II era and the Marxism of Stalin's time—exist not merely as abstract theories but as embodied political forces. In such an environment, the theological idealist is often forced to take sides, to throw in his lot with one or another active organization. In many places there are few organized alternatives of the middle, democratic way.

Thus it was that in 1968, the second Conference of Latin American Bishops at Medellín legitimized not only the normal preaching of the Church about social conscience ("the formation of Christian conscience") and not only the classical, peaceful tactics of social reform (labor unions, credit unions, cooperatives, and the like), but also the bald use of Marxist categories. It did so in a context in which instances of armed insurrection by a few "guerrilla priests"—not simply as chaplains but as active combatants—were occurring, and in which the public-policy elites of the continent, especially the university intelligentsia, were already deeply immersed in Marxist thought.

But in what sense are the liberation theologians Marxist? None of them shows evidence that he has actually studied Marx, the social systems derived from Marxist thought, or the literature assessing socialist experiments. They do not, apparently, believe in the total abolition of private property (the principle Marx offered as a pithy summary of his theory). They claim not to be materialists. They are not atheists. They say that they are not totalitarians, as Castro is. They surely do not hold—since few Marxists today do—that economic gains for the poor are empirically to be achieved through the nationalization of major industries. It is doubtful whether they believe in the humane quality of the authoritarian, bureaucratic state which is the natural outgrowth of socialism. It is not clear that they are ready to impose equality, to command choices of what society and individuals "need," to insist upon planning by technical experts, or to repress private initiatives.

Nevertheless, there do seem to be two senses in which they are Marxists. Repeatedly, liberation theologians insist that they are Marxists "because the people are." By this they do not mean that "the people" have ever read Marx or know much about him but a few slogans. But the slogans are the point. If it is difficult to take liberation theologians seriously as theoreticians of Marxism, one can grant that they are "populist Marxists," using Marxist slogans to ventilate some of the frustrations and aggressions of people whose aspirations have long been colored by external propaganda.

There is a second sense in which they are Marxists. Marxism in Latin America is not just a theory. It is a well-financed, well-organized political institution, with parties, officials, printing presses, secret agents, operatives, intellectual sympathizers, international connections, and designated politicians. To be a Marxist, as the liberation theologians say, is not merely to hold a theory but to be committed to a "praxis." Yet the innocence with which the liberation theologians are committed to the Marxist "praxis" speaks volumes.

Marxist "praxis" is something of which the world has had some experience—but one would not know it from the writings of the liberation theologians. The literature of liberation theology, which is rich in general allegations about "capitalist" practice, is silent when it comes to the empirical evidence of how Marxist regimes operate. Since almost three-quarters of the world's nations are, officially, Marxist in design, and since most have had upward of thirty years to prove themselves, it should not have been beyond the capacity of theologians to work out an assessment, even a theological assessment, of their actual daily "praxis," and judge these in the light of the gospels. But this the liberation theologians have conspicuously not done.

The Missing Measurements

In recounting the experience of the "poor and the oppressed" of the Third World, strange gaps appear in the empirical reasoning of liberation theologians. No notice is taken of those Third World nations whose annual rate of economic growth borders on 10 per cent—nations like Taiwan, Hong Kong, South Korea, Singapore, whose secrets in overcoming poverty are open to inspection. No empirical survey of the comparative inequalities between elites and the poor is made as between socialist and capitalist regimes. Little attention is paid to measurements of institutional respect for human dignity and liberties, as, for example, between South Korea and North Korea.

There are other strange gaps in empirical knowledge. Bishop Helder Camara, in his youth a Fascist as in his maturity a Marxist, is constant in his criticism of liberal democracies. He is especially fond of the suggestion that a small fraction of mankind uses a large fraction of the earth's resources, and that poverty results for millions. Is this in fact true? A special kind of human culture is required for the production of wealth. Not every organization of society or culture is suited to such production. Indeed, only a small fraction of the earth's population *produces* the larger part of the world's wealth. Besides, many of the earth's resources were unknown even a century ago, or no use for them—hence no value—had yet been found. In fact, Latin America is immensely rich in resources, now that other cultures have discovered their secrets and learned their uses.

It is not empirically true, either, that "the poor are getting poorer." In longevity, medical care, and nutrition, the modern production of wealth has raised the levels of the entire population of the world by unprecedented annual increments over the last fifty years. Average personal incomes have also risen annually, in Latin America even more than in Asia or Africa. If the present organization of the production of wealth is "sinful," what shall we say of rival Marxist systems, which are not raising the levels of the poor by so much?

Catholic theologians, especially those who claim to speak for "liberation," have a duty to study how liberation has, in fact, been attained in human history, and by what empirical and practical means its scope can be extended. If such a study were undertaken dispassionately and in good faith, I believe it would show that the greatest chances for improving the concrete daily life of human beings everywhere lie not with the forces of Marxist "liberation" but with the forces of democratic capitalism. Others may disagree; but that Catholic social theory has so far failed even to raise the necessary intellectual questions is a sign of its bankruptcy in this area, and of the extent to which too much of it has, in fact, already fallen hostage to Marxist categories of thought.

In the writings of liberation theologians, the contradictions of Marxist theory and practice go unnoted. And this tells us something about the liberation theologians: they are Marxists not by reason or by experience, but by faith. As Leszek Kolakowski, who (like Pope John Paul II) has lived though the Marxist phenomenon in Poland, has observed: "Almost all the prophecies of Marx and his followers have already proved to be false, but this does not disturb the spiritual certainty of the faithful, any more than it did in the case of chiliastic sects: for it is a certainty not based on any empirical premises or supposed 'historical laws,' but simply on the psychological need for certainty. In this sense Marxism performs the function of a religion, and its efficacy is of a religious character."

In the real world, Marxism has been immobilized for decades as the ideological superstructure of totalitarian states and of parties aspiring to that status. As an explanatory system, Marxism "explains" little. There is nothing in the Latin American system, to which the liberation theologians point, for which Marxism affords the only or the best explanation. It offers no "method" either of inquiry or of action by which modern life is to be better understood, its future predicted, or its utopian hopes realized. Contemporary Marxist literature, as Kolakowski shows, is dogmatic, sterile, helpless, out of touch both with modern economics and with cultural life. But what Marxism does do very well today is to inspire with fantasies of utopian fulfillment, and to license the identification of some malevolent enemy as the only roadblock to that fulfillment. In a quite literal sense, the works of liberation theologians are innocent both of empirical verification and of sophistication about Marxist theory. Their originality lies chiefly in their openness to fantasy.

It is thus hardly surprising that Pope John Paul II's clear-eyed account of Marxism in Puebla proved to have a stronger bite than many Catholics could accept. He attempted to staunch the unthinking fantasies of theologians bent on the creation of totalitarian processes whose consequences they do not allow themselves to foresee and whose dynamics they cannot control. As against this, the Pope maintained the independence and integrity of the Church. He based himself on sound political philosophy. He spoke for the authentic interests of the poor and the oppressed, against those who would transmute their sufferings into envy, hatred, and coercion. He refused to adopt the role of Dostoevsky's Grand Inquisitor, offering bread in exchange for liberty. For this, even those who are secular have reason to be grateful.

JAMES V. SCHALL, S.J.

The American Press Views Puebla

THOUGH PERHAPS NOT FULLY EVIDENT when John Paul II
arrived at Puebla in January 1979, it became quite clear during the
rest of his Mexican trip and later in Poland and on other trips that
the Pope is the most prominent religious (if not political) personality in the world today.[1] His popularity has turned aside the criticism
normally reserved for religious leaders, that nobody listens to
them. As many have noted, John Paul is a living refutation of what
Stalin implied in his contemptuous question, "How many divisions
does the Pope have?" Evidently, the Pope's legions increase as
anti-Christian efforts to eliminate them increase.

Within the Church, too, this powerful personality has put into
some disarray a growing theological prejudice that pretended the
"true" Church was with the theologians and clergy, who supposedly had the exclusive ear of "the poor," of the masses of the
world. John Paul quickly proved that if anyone had the poor in his
hand, it was he. Thus he deftly managed to put on the intellectual
defensive not only the radicals within the Church but also the
radical humanists and Marxists—and this on their own terms of "to
whom do the poor really listen?" This is significant for North
America as well as for Latin America.

*James V. Schall, S.J., is an associate professor of government at
Georgetown University, Washington, D.C. He is a consultor to the
Pontifical Commission on Justice and Peace. Among his books are
"Christianity and Politics" and "Liberation Theology."*

86

North American politicians and intellectuals are vaguely beginning to grasp what their training in law and political science never
taught them: that in the modern world ignorance of religion is a
major form of political and journalistic ineptitude.[2] Therefore, the
Mexican visit of John Paul II was watched with some perplexity by
the American secular press, which, as if aware of its ignorance in
this area, covered the Holy Father's visit much more thoroughly
than President Carter's visit to Mexico two weeks later.[3]

Rather often in the American press, however, the Pope's visit to
the Puebla Conference of Latin American Bishops was described
as a kind of clerical version of *The Shoot-Out at the O.K. Corral,*
with John Paul demonstrating the fastest draw in the West. What
had seeped north during recent years, largely through the leftist
dogmas flowing unceasingly from such sources as the Maryknoll
Order's Orbis Press and abetted by a generation of economically
ignorant Protestant and Catholic missionaries serving in Latin
America, was that perhaps Marx was right after all—spruced up a
bit, of course. Guilt-ridden missionaries from the United States
were advised to return home to preach the Latin revolutionary
gospel in Pittsburgh, provincial curias, and Harvard, where it presumably would do some good. Not surprisingly, the universities
and the religious orders were more susceptible to this sort of thing
than workers in Pittsburgh.

The drama of Christians, in the name of faith, embracing the
contemporary ideology most heretical to Christianity was
heightened by the arrival of a new pope who had lived under actual
Marxist rule. Theologians whose writings betrayed their ignorance
of how Marxist states really operate (despite the vast literature and
testimony available to inform them) were confronted by a pope
who had no doubts at all about just how such states function. The
desperate pleas that somehow Latin American Marxism is "different" seemed less and less credible.

What was particularly noteworthy in the reporting and analysis
of papal statements in the American press was the persistent
failure—there were exceptions, of course—to grasp the specifically religious import of the Pope's message. Writers for the leading American newspapers and journals, themselves often infected

with the ideological bias of secular humanism, seemed unable to conceive of the reality of religion in any but economic and political terms. For example: "If there is a common aspect among all these elements [of the Pope's personality]," wrote Tad Szulc of the later Polish visit, "it is John Paul's utter obsession with the terrestrial destiny and dignity of the human being. He speaks infrequently of the hereafter, or of the immortal soul: it is man on earth, always man, who concerns him—man's human rights, his mental processes, and his sexuality and sensuality in holy matrimony."[4]

Turnabout in the Press

The most "secular" and "liberal" of the American press, including many elements in the Catholic press, went through a fascinating about-face as John Paul's immense popularity became undeniably clear. The initial tone was critical. The early *New York Times* editorial—one about which it seems to have had some second thoughts, to judge from subsequent news articles[5]—was most curious as a piece of American secular ideology ("A Voice Against 'Liberation Theology,' " January 30, 1979). How is one to analyze its underlying sympathies when, on the matter of social activism with a Marxist orientation, a pope is chided for not being more enthusiastic about a movement that, on other grounds, the *Times* itself would have opposed vigorously? This reveals a willingness to abandon the possibility that in the question of how to help the poor, American and classic Catholic social thought might represent a third alternative (i.e., neither Marxism nor nineteenth-century capitalism). It also reveals a willful incapacity to grasp specifically religious values.

Without much analysis of the real significance of "liberation theology," the *Times* editorial pictured the Pope as rejecting it totally. Apparently, as the *Times* read the Pope's meaning, the Church was supposed to pray and say pious things, but not to act. "It was a disappointing speech." And so the *Times* ended its analysis with the kind of dogmatic liberalism that Pius IX rightly worried about in the last century: "But some in the Church are asking how priests can minister to spiritual needs of their depressed and neglected people without somehow working to alleviate the conditions that oppress them. It is a good question." In the *Times* view, religion is useful insofar as it aids politics and economics. In other contexts, no doubt, this same liberalism would argue that church and state ought to be separated. Thus the *Times* did not applaud John Paul when he insisted on teaching religion in state schools in Poland, for such thoughts are dangerous to the American liberal. Liberation theology and American secular liberal thought are in a certain way bedfellows: both rely on certain basic absolutist principles.

Colman McCarthy took up this same line of thought in the *Washington Post* ("Papal Blandness," February 3, 1979). Setting aside any scriptural interpretations other than the Marxist-influenced ones provided by the liberation theologians, he stated that biblical scholars "commonly stress the revolutionary role that Christ assumed in secular society—he incited people against the state religion and against paying taxes. . . ." The fact that Christ told his disciples to *pay* taxes and to put away the sword makes one wonder just what version of the Bible McCarthy had been reading. The only thing revolutionary about the cleansing in the Temple was the insistence that religion be something besides commerce and politics. McCarthy went on to say: "Hopes were raised before Puebla that, even though John Paul had the bent of a doctrinal traditionalist, at least his social and political views would be liberal: that was true of John XXIII and Paul VI. But the hopes appear to be unfounded for John Paul II."

But when the implications of such analyses became publicized and the surprising popularity of John Paul II among the very poor became known, a sudden caution appeared. Many of those who had expressed critical views of Puebla became uneasy. And so the Pope's message had to be reinterpreted—"read again more carefully," as it was said—so as to be seen not as a criticism of the Latin American church in the social activist role endorsed by the previous bishops' conference (Medellín, 1968) but only as a mild reprimand for certain quite understandable "aberrations." In this vein Dean Peerman wrote in the *Christian Century:* "A close reading of the text, however, suggests that John Paul II was rejecting not liberation theology per se but certain extreme forms of it which tend to transmute the gospel into political ideology, and whose adherents look upon all-out class warfare, and even Castro-style revolution, as the only way to achieve social justice."[6] The Pope was said to have changed between the first speech and his last; supposedly, liberal bishops had gotten to him to explain "the facts" of Latin America.

The *National Catholic Reporter* and the *Nation*—which had the same reporter covering the conference (Penny Lernoux)—took up this view by attacking the earlier "interpretations" of John Paul's intent.[7] Harvey Cox, writing in *Commonweal,* made this astonishing analysis of Puebla:

> What is really tearing up Latin America, disrupting families, undermining cherished values, widening the gulf between rich and poor is not Marxism, and certainly not the Catholic left, but consumer capitalism. I am once again confirmed in my opinion . . . that the Christian socialists of Latin America are the real 'conservatives'. . . ."[8]

What this implies is that socialism is not an ideology of change—which the Latin American revolutionaries presumably really desire—but a way to control society to prevent the kind of change that would bring freedom and abundance to the Latin American masses. Radical-chic socialism thus finds itself opposed, in the name of religion, to giving people who need something to consume a system that in fact produces consumable things.

Arthur Jones, then editor of the *National Catholic Reporter,* wrote that the Pope "certainly understands that from a Christian perspective, capitalism and communism are equally bad."[9] There is, of course, no evidence at all that the Pope "understands" this. Although classical liberalism has been condemned along with classical Marxism in the papal encyclicals, it is clear that the latter is considered worse than the former. This advice from Jones could only amuse the Pope: "The Pope has to be able to accept that the Marxist experience in Latin America is not the Marxist experience in Eastern Europe; in the latter case, Marxism is the mask for totalitarianism; in Latin America, it is not—though it could develop that way." And of course, if it did, would not the Church be responsible if it had aided and abetted the "Marxist experience"? This is the real danger of liberation analysis, as the Pope sees it.

Rescuing a Noble Word

The Pope's tactic was, then, to rescue the noble word "liberation" from the Marxist and sociological categories in which it has been formulated and to restore its Christian religious and transcendent setting. This was what Paul VI had set out to do in his 1975 statement on evangelization, *Evangelii Nuntiandi*. John Paul II, from his Polish background, is quite aware of the effort to reduce the Christian faith to a purely spiritual sphere, something that intellectually goes back to the fourteenth-century political philosopher Marsilius of Padua. But in Latin America he confronts an ideology that seeks to do the opposite, to reidentify throne and altar, this time with a left rather than a politically right basis.

Another mode of presenting the Pope's message was that represented by the Catholic journals *America* and *Commonweal*. In a way, it seems strange that the Catholic center-left echoed so closely the *New York Times* and the *Los Angeles Times*. *Commonweal*'s editorial, for example, suggested that John Paul was unable to distinguish between a Poland or a Rome and Latin America. A liberation theologian was cited at length to the effect that Jesus, by following his own religious methods, changed society in its structure and that therefore changing structures is an active part of religion. Jesus was said to have "denounced all privilege and inequality before the common fatherhood of God"—this despite his parable of the talents and his assertion that "many are called, but few are chosen." The editorial concluded:

> If he [John Paul] had taken this emphasis [that political commitment was integral rather than secondary to the life of faith], he would have given Latin American theology and evangelization a clear direction. As it is, the progressive bishops will go ahead and institutionalize the guidelines originally set by Medellín ten years ago, but only half-sure they have the Holy Father's blessing.[10]

The question remains whether half a blessing is better than none.

Evidently Medellín is thought to interpret the papacy, rather than the reverse.

America, likewise, wrote: "If the Pope's message to the bishops of Latin America was disappointing, it was more the result of what he did not say than what he said. . . . He was strangely silent about hundreds of Catholics who have been imprisoned, tortured, and killed by Latin American governments because of their commitment to the vision the Pope now called his own."[11] This is an oft-repeated line, one requiring critical reflection in the context of the Pope's admonition not to use certain methods. To have done what the *America* editors suggested would, of course, have been to contradict the very purpose of the papal message. Many of the clergy in Latin America who have been "suppressed" in various ways have been so treated because they embraced the kind of radical *political* activity that, for clergy, the Pope is against.

Latin American dictators are probably quite aware of the likely political consequences of clerical political successes, consequences that the clerics do not foresee. By not encouraging political martyrdom in the name of religion, the Pope was saying that the ways of politics are other than ways of religious witness. And he insisted that these other ways are not merely arbitrary for the Christian, and especially not for the cleric. No doubt some are persecuted unjustly, but not all. And again, if Christian martyrdom and suffering in the past, even as inflicted by political oppressors, is any criterion, these acts were not to be seen in solely political terms.

Louis Fleming, in the *Los Angeles Times,* brought up the question that is most crucial in this context, that of specifics: What are the alternatives proposed?[12] Liberation theology is itself a very vague ideology in this regard, deliberately so (as Michael Novak pointed out in the perceptive essay that is in this volume), particularly in its inability to compare the actual performance record of existing examples of socialism and Marxism to the actual record of democratic capitalism. The vast outpourings of liberation thought speak of Marxism as if it had never yet existed and of capitalism as if we were still trying to repeal the Corn Laws in nineteenth-century England.

What then does the Pope really offer? Szulc wrote:

> Others think that the Pope, enormously influenced by his expe-
> rience under the communist regime in Poland, but, nevertheless,
> disenchanted with the workings of capitalism as he has observed
> it during his many world trips, is searching—perhaps groping—
> for a new body of philosophy that would interpose itself between
> Marxism and capitalism.[13]

The Pope is challenged to come up with a "plan" for the world, as if
he were a politician, something classical Christian social thought
has been most careful to warn against, precisely because religion is
not politics.

And significantly, the "specifics" the Pope did come up with—
the religious ones—were often ignored because of the liberal and
Marxist ideological bias and the tendency to avoid the reality of
faith itself. The Pope's Polish experience is doubly important in
this regard, for, as Leopold Tyrmand pointed out, the "political"
strength of religion depends on its own internal discipline and
doctrine, something John Paul stressed to the U.S. bishops.[14]

In this connection, the *New York Times* editorial on John Paul's
Polish visit was revealing. Apparently the *Times* believed that in
Poland the strengthening of religion is *not* meant to upset the
established political order, whereas in Latin America it is.

> The speeches of John Paul II call for greater freedom for the
> Church, for greater opportunity to educate the Polish young and
> for greater Church participation in determining Poland's future.
> But these are far less than the summons to end communist rule
> or to break with Marxism. As much as the visit of John Paul II to
> Poland must reinvigorate and reinspire the Roman Catholic
> Church in Poland, it does not threaten the political order of the
> nations of Eastern Europe.[15]

The *Times* expressed no admonition that priests in Poland be
active for an exploited people, no hint about the injustice of the
existing regime, but only a kind of relief that the status quo would
remain unthreatened.

A final series of views in the American press seem more perceptive of the religious importance of the present papal stance. The
Wall Street Journal wrote:

Governments lacking moral sanction are in danger no matter what armies they command.

The issue of moral sanction is very much at the heart of the struggle in Latin America as well. It is quite likely true that the Roman Church has at times in the past too willingly contributed moral authority to regimes that little deserve its support. Priests and bishops with genuine sympathy for the aspirations of the Latin masses undoubtedly will carry the future of the Church in that part of the world.

But it would be a tragedy if the Latin priests and bishops failed to see the crucial points where Marxism and Christianity are antithetical. . . . It would hardly seem beyond possibility that the Church could bring its moral authority on Latin governments without aligning itself with Marxist revolution.[16]

This is one of the more discerning comments, but again the question is whether a nineteenth-century "capitalism" and a visionary, non-existent Marxism are really the only alternatives.

Dale Vree, writing in *National Review,* paid special attention to the theological implications of liberation doctrine, which holds that (1) the Church is a sign of universal salvation, (2) whose main task is to bring the world to its intended perfection, (3) and this by siding with the poor and oppressed.

With such ecclesiology, doctrinal truth about God and Christ ("orthodoxy") is of no consequence, since according to the heterodox doctrine of universal salvation, everyone will be saved regardless of what he believes or does. But the Pope countered that argument head-on: "to be watchful for purity of doctrine . . . is . . . together with the proclamation of the Gospel, the primary and irreplaceable duty" of the Church. The claim that the Church's mission is, like that of the Marxist parties, to perfect the world trades on a fundamental misunderstanding of the Kingdom of God.[17]

Leopold Tyrmand wrote in this same vein in the *Wall Street Journal:* John Paul understands the essential importance of intelligence in the Church, that "the Christian weapon—faith—is useless today without a philosophical dimension and that Catholic personalism, the belief that humans transcend sociopolitical conditioning, is the center of the global struggle."[18]

What these varying analyses of John Paul's Mexican addresses make clear is not simply the nature of the real intellectual and religious struggle of our era—whether man is exclusively humanist, a product of his own or nature's making—but also the nature of any genuine approach to concrete aid to the poor of Latin America and the rest of the Third World. It is not the Pope but his critics who lack "specifics." The thrust of liberation theology is very clear: to impose on Latin America another absolutist system, one that controls but does not lessen scarcity through a collective loss of freedom, usually called socialism.

Ignoring a Third Way

No one has to agree that the current economic systems of Latin America are ideal. What few notice is that it is the capitalists themselves who tell us this. To the degree that Latin economic practice is not related to the kind of democratic capitalism that could in fact do what everyone wants done—feed and clothe and house and liberate the poor—it needs to be reformed.[19] The proposed reformation will not do what the liberationists want. There is, in other words, room for a third reality that is never treated in the discussion, even by American liberals, who persist in joining the either/or of Latin Marxism or Latin capitalism.

The failure of a third way—for Catholics, it probably had its roots in the rejection of Jacques Maritain's *Reflections on America*—indicates the decline in Catholic social thought from its own central tradition and its current inability to recognize relatively successful economic and political values and structures.[20] Latin Americans, to their credit, do recognize that North American secularism, often under the guise of aid to the poor in the form of population control or statist theory, represents values and practices that limit freedom and demean the human person. The Pope's visit reveals most of all the genuine need to present a democratic capitalism devoid of both the secularist presumptions of liberal humanism and the mythology of the Marxist distortion of capitalism.

John Paul II did an enormous service at Puebla by insisting that religion remain a transcendent value free from ideological attempts to harness it exclusively to the world of economics and politics. Moreover, as a Polish Christian he was in a prophetic position to see that, in confronting a Marxist or liberal absolutist system, the essential things that Christians need are their own faith, their own pulpits, their own discipline. And these are not primarily political. The effort to "save Medellín" by implying that John Paul's views, if read carefully, say nothing different misses the whole significance of his analysis. And it does so precisely because most analyses of Medellín identified religion and politics too closely, jeopardizing the authenticity of both spheres.

What seems most striking about the ideological trend of "identifying with the poor" is, then, a paucity of insight into how the poor were ever aided in the first place. In retrospect, the Medellín approach seems more like a mystical identification than a political or economic program for the real poor. It seems rather dubious to tell poor people that some kind of spiritual togetherness with Christian elites is, at this level, more important than plans that might actually put more food on their tables.

Puebla did in this sense correct Medellín. What remains to be seen is whether Latin intellectuals can understand anything other than a Hegel or a Marx. If they cannot, John Paul's trip was in vain.

PART FOUR

Puebla Confirmed

That John Paul II intended his Puebla address to mean what it said was made clear in many of his subsequent statements. In a general audience in Rome on February 21, 1979, the Pope explained his understanding of Christian "liberation" in these words: "Christ himself links liberation particularly with knowledge of the truth: 'You will know the truth, and the truth will make you free' (John 8:32). . . . Liberation means man's inner transformation, which is a consequence of the knowledge of truth. The transformation is, therefore, a spiritual process, in which man matures 'in true righteousness and holiness' (Eph. 4:24). Man, inwardly mature in this way, becomes a representative and a spokesman of this 'righteousness' in the various environments of social life" (*L'Osservatore Romano,* February 26, 1979). This statement excludes the use of the Church as a political instrument but emphasizes the *personal* social-political responsibilities of the Christian. The same theme was strikingly presented on July 19, 1981, in the Pope's Angelus message:

> The Christian cannot, certainly, expect to find in the Eucharist ready-made suggestions about the action to be carried out in the various fields of his personal, family, social or communitarian, economic or political life. Participation in the "Lord's Supper" always concerns closely, however, his awareness of good and evil, and places before him his own responsibilities with regard to persons near or far away, with regard to the world around him. Therefore, communion in the "bread broken" commits each one to make his own contribution to the building of a "new world" [*L'Osservatore Romano,* July 27, 1981].

Again, and very clearly, we see his rejection of the concept of the Church as a political instrument or the Christian ethic as a guidebook on specific policy questions. He places the moral responsibility squarely on the Christ-informed person as citizen rather than on some presumed Church Political.

It was in Africa and Brazil, however, that John Paul II most vividly pointed to the limits of formal church structures in the political arena. In his remarks to the priests of Zaire, the Pope summarized their positive role—their competences, so to speak—as performing the eucharistic sacrifice, renewing the sacrifice of the cross; preaching the Gospel and catechetics; administering all sacraments; and constituting a point of unity. Against this background, the following statement is powerful: "Leave political responsibilities to those who are charged with them: You have another part, a magnificent part, you are 'leaders' by another right and in another manner. . . . Your sphere of interventions, and it is vast, is that of faith and morals. . . ."

Finally, that John Paul II is in the mainstream of modest assertions, and is offering a corrective to political excesses in the name of the Church, was most powerfully established in his several addresses in Brazil in July 1980. At Vidigal, the Rio slum where he gave his gold ring to the local parish: "In this evangelical fight [to help develop social conscience and concern for the poor] the church of the poor will not serve immediate political purposes or power struggles. She tries at the same time with great care to ensure that her words and actions are not used for the purpose, that is, 'instrumentalized.' "

Such clear disavowals of political pretense are sometimes portrayed as "conservative" reactions to "liberal" or "radical" traditions in recent church teachings. This is a false categorization. John Paul II's admonitions to develop social conscience and consciousness, to help people, to share wealth and promote the common good, are at least as urgently and passionately put as those of any of his predecessors. He is not retreating on any basic issues of human welfare, but he places severe limits on the claims of the Church to be a political actor and the claims of anyone to invoke the Church's authority in specific political decisions.

Thus "the Church will respect the competence of public authorities in these matters. It will not claim to intervene in politics; it will not aspire to share in managing temporal affairs. Its specific contribution will be to fortify the spiritual and moral bases of society by doing what is possible for all or any activity in the field of the common good." The Church's service "is above all a service of formation of consciences" (remarks at Salvador, Brazil).

For any who thought that perhaps John Paul II's Puebla address was an aberration or that he was "open to interpretation" on religion and politics, his comments in Africa and Brazil, major portions of which follow, *should* have put the issue to rest.

JOHN PAUL II

Be Pastors,
Not Politicians

Address to Priests,
Kinshasa, Zaire
May 4, 1980

DEAR BROTHER PRIESTS,

1. I have eagerly desired this meeting with you. Priests, as you know, have a special place in my heart and in my prayer. That is normal: With you, I am a priest. He who has been established as the pastor of the whole flock has his eyes fixed first of all on those who share his pastorate, which is the pastorate of Christ, on those who daily bear "the burden of the day and of the heat." And your mission is so important for the Church.

Last year, for Holy Thursday, I addressed a special letter to all the priests of the world, through the intermediacy of their bishops. In the name of the whole Church, I expressed to you my sentiments of gratitude and confidence. I reminded you of your priestly identity, in relation to Christ the priest, to the good shepherd. I situated your ministry in the Church. I also showed the meaning of the requirements attached to your priestly state. I hope that you have read that letter, that you will reread it. I cannot take up again here all its themes, even briefly. I shall rather offer several thoughts which extend it. I intend above all to speak to you personally, priests in Africa, priests in Zaire. This is one of my first meetings on African soil, a privileged meeting with my brother priests.

Reprinted from "Origins" (published by the National Catholic News Service), May 22, 1980.

2. Beyond your persons, I think of all the priests of the African continent. Of those who have come from afar for the beginnings of evangelization and who continue to bring their precious and indispensable aid. I do not dare to say "missionaries" too much, for all must be missionaries. And I think also—and most especially in the present conversation—of the priests who have come forth from the African peoples: They are already a response rich in consoling promises; they are the most convincing demonstration of the maturity which your young churches have attained; they are already, and they are called more and more to be, its leaders. They are particularly numerous in this country. That is a great grace for which we thank God, in this centenary of evangelization. It is also a great responsibility.

3. Among so many thoughts which crowd in my soul at this moment, which shall I choose as the theme of this meeting? It seems to me that the best subject is provided to us by the apostle Paul, when he exhorts his disciple Timothy to revive the gift that God placed in him by the imposition of the hands (cf. 2 Tim. 1:6), and to draw, from a conscience renewed by this grace, the courage to pursue with generosity the path undertaken, because "it is not a spirit of fear that God has given us, but a spirit of strength, of love and of self-mastery" (1:7).

Our meditation today must therefore begin by recalling the fundamental characteristics of the priesthood. To be a priest means to be a mediator between God and men, in the mediator par excellence who is Christ.

Jesus was able to accomplish his mission thanks to his total union with the Father, because he was one with him: in his condition as pilgrim on the roads of our earth *(viator),* he was already in possession of the goal *(comprehensor)* to which he had to lead others. To be able to continue effectively the mission of Christ, the priest must in some way himself have already arrived where he wants to lead others. He arrives there by diligent contemplation of the mystery of God, nourished by the study of Scripture, a study which expands into prayer.

Fidelity to the moments and means of personal prayer, the more official prayer of the hours, but also the worthy and generous carrying out of the sacred acts of the ministry, contributes to sanctify the priest and to lead him to an experience of the mysterious and fascinating presence of the living God, while permitting him to act forcefully on the human environment surrounding him.

4. Christ especially exercised his office as mediator by the immolation of his life in the sacrifice of the cross, accepted through obedience to the Father. The cross remains the "obligatory" route of meeting with God. It is a road on which the priest first of all must launch himself courageously. As I recalled in my recent letter on the eucharist, is he not called to renew *in persona Christi,* in the eucharistic celebration, the sacrifice of the cross? According to the beautiful expression of the African Augustine of Hippo, Christ on Calvary was "priest and sacrifice, and therefore priest because sacrifice" (*Confessions,* X, 43, 69). The priest who, in the radical poverty of obedience to God, to the Church, to his bishop will have known how to make his life a pure offering to offer, in union with Christ, to the heavenly Father, will experience in his ministry the victorious strength of the grace of Christ who has died and risen.

As a mediator, the Lord Jesus was, in all the dimensions of his being, the man for God and for the brothers. Likewise the priest, and that's the reason for which he is asked to consecrate his whole life to God and to the Church, in the depths of his being, of his faculties, of his sentiments. The priest who, in the choice of celibacy, renounces human love to be opened totally to that of God, makes himself free to be given to men by a gift excluding no one, but including them all in the flow of charity which comes from God (cf. Rom. 5:5) and leads to God. Celibacy, in linking the priest to God, frees him for all the works required by the care of souls.

There you have sketched in several characteristics the essential physiognomy of the priest, such as it has been left to us by the venerable tradition of the Church. It has a permanent value, yesterday, today, tomorrow. It is not a matter of ignoring the new problems posed by the contemporary world, and also by the African context, for it is important to prepare priests who may be at the same time fully African and authentically Christian. The questions posed by the culture into which the priestly ministry is inserted demand mature reflection. But it is in any case in the light of the fundamental theology which I have recalled that they must be approached and resolved.

6. * It is not necessary now that I speak extensively about the different functions of the priest. You have meditated upon, you must often take up again, the texts of the Second Vatican Council, the Dogmatic Constitution on the Church (section 28) and the whole Decree on the Ministry and Life of Priests.

The preaching of the Gospel, of the whole Gospel, to each category of Christians and also to non-Christians, must take a great place in your life. The faithful have a right to it. On this ministry of the Word of God catechesis especially depends, which must be able to touch the heart and the mind of your fellow countrymen, and the formation of catechists, religious and lay. And be educators of the faith and of Christian life, according to the Church, in personal, family, professional spheres.

The worthy celebration of the sacraments, the dispensing of the mysteries of God, is also central in your life as priests. In this area, watch diligently over the preparation of the faithful to receive them, so that, for example, the sacraments of baptism, of penance, of the eucharist, of marriage, may bear all their fruits.

For Christ exercises the force of his redemptive action in the sacraments. He does it particularly in the eucharist and in the sacrament of penance.

The apostle Paul said: "God . . . has entrusted to us the ministry of reconciliation" (2 Cor. 5:19). The people of God are called to a continual conversion, to an ever renewed reconciliation with God in Christ. This reconciliation is effected in the sacrament of penance, and it is there that you exercise, par excellence, your ministry of reconciliation.

Yes, the Pope knows your difficulties: You have so many pastoral tasks to perform and you never have enough time. But each Christian has a right, yes, a right to a personal meeting with

---

*There is no section 5 in the original published text. — ED.

the crucified Christ who pardons. And, as I said in my first encyclical, "it is evident that it is a matter at the same time of a right of Christ himself with regard to each man whom he has redeemed" (*Redemptor Hominis,* 20). That is why I beg you: Always consider this ministry of reconciliation in the sacrament of penance one of your most important tasks.

Finally, the "spiritual power" which has been given to you (cf. Decree on the Ministry and Life of Priests, 6) has been given to build up the Church, to lead it like the Lord, the good shepherd, with a humble and unselfish devotion, always hospitable, with an availability to assume the various ministries and services that are necessary and complementary in the unity of the presbyterate, with a great concern for collaboration among yourselves, priests, and with your bishops. The Christian people must be led to unity in seeing the fraternal love and cohesion that you manifest. Your authority in the exercise of your functions is linked to your fidelity to the Church which is entrusted to you. Leave political responsibilities to those who are charged with them: You have another part, a magnificent part, you are "leaders" by another right and in another manner, participating in the priesthood of Christ, as his ministers. Your sphere of interventions, and it is vast, is that of faith and morals, where it is expected that you preach at the same time by a courageous word and by the example of your life.

7. Each member of the Church has an irreplaceable role in it. Yours also consists in helping all those who belong to your communities to fill theirs, brothers, sisters, laity. You have especially to bring to fulfillment that of the laity: It must never be forgotten, indeed, that baptism and confirmation confer a specific responsibility in the Church. I therefore enthusiastically approve your concern to raise up collaborators, to form them to their responsibilities. Yes, it is necessary to know how to tirelessly address direct, concrete, precise appeals to them. It is necessary to form them by making them aware of the hidden riches that they bear in themselves. It is necessary finally to really know how to collaborate, without monopolizing all the tasks, all the initiatives, or all the decisions, when it concerns what is in the area of their competence and their responsibility. It is thus that living communities are formed, which truly represent a picture of the primitive Church, in which one sees appear, around the apostle, the names of these numerous auxiliaries, men and women, whom St. Paul greets as his "co-workers in Christ Jesus" (Rom. 16:3).

8. In all this pastoral work, the inevitable difficulties must not damage our confidence. *Scimus Christum surrexisse a mortuis vere* (We know that Christ has really risen from the dead). The presence of the risen Christ is a sure basis for a hope "which does not deceive" (Mark 5:5). That is why the priest must be, always and everywhere, a man of hope. It is indeed true that the world is crisscrossed by profound tensions, which often give rise to difficulties whose immediate solution is beyond us. In such circumstances, and at all times, the priest must know how to offer convincing reasons for hope to his brothers, by word and example. And he can do it because his certitudes are not based on human opinions, but on the solid rock of the Word of God.

9. Sustained by it, the priest must reveal himself to be a man of discernment and an authentic teacher of the faith.

Yes, he must be, especially in our times, a man of discernment. For, as we all know, if the modern world has made great progress in the area of knowledge and human development, it is also full of a great number of ideologies and pseudo-values which, through a fallacious language, too often succeed in seducing and deceiving many of our contemporaries. Not only must we know how not to succumb to that, obviously, but the function of pastors is also to form the Christian judgment of the faithful (cf. 1 Tim. 5:21; 1 John 4:1), so that they may be themselves also capable of withdrawing themselves from the deceitful fascination of these new "idols."

In that, the priest will also reveal himself to be an authentic teacher of the faith. He will lead Christians to mature in their faith, by communicating to them an ever deeper knowledge of the gospel message—"not their own wisdom, but the word of God" (cf. Decree on the Ministry and Life of Priests, 4)—and by helping them to judge the circumstances of life in its light. Thus, thanks to your persevering efforts, today, in Africa, Catholics will know how to discover the answers which, in full fidelity to the unchanging values of tradition, will also be capable of satisfying in an adequate manner the needs and questions of the present.

10. I have recalled the role of all the faithful in the Church. But, at the end of this conversation, I draw your attention to the primordial duty that you have with regard to vocations. The meaning of the whole Christian vocation is so intimately dependent on that of the priestly vocation that, in Christian communities where the latter disappears, the very authenticity of the Christian life would be damaged. Work tirelessly therefore, dear brothers, to make the whole people of God understand the importance of vocations. Pray and have others pray for that; help those called to the priesthood or the religious life to discern the signs of their vocation; support them throughout their formation. You are indeed convinced that the future of the Church will depend on holy priests, because the priesthood belongs to the structure of the Church as Christ has willed it. Finally, dear brothers, do you not believe that the Lord will first of all make use of the example of our own lives, generous and radiant, to raise up other vocations?

11. Very dear brothers, have faith in your priesthood. It is the everlasting priesthood, because it is a participation in the eternal priesthood of Christ, "who is the same yesterday, today and forever" (Heb. 13:8; cf. Rev. 1:17 ff.). Yes, if the demands of the priesthood are indeed great, and if I have nevertheless not hesitated to speak to you about them, it is because they are only the consequence of the nearness of the Lord, of the confidence he has in his priests. "I no longer call you my servants, but I call you my friends" (John 15:15). This song of the day of our ordination remains for each of you, as it does for me, a permanent source of joy and confidence. It is that joy which I invite you to renew today. May the Virgin Mary always be your support on the way, and may she introduce us all more each day into the intimacy of the Lord. With my affectionate apostolic blessing.

JOHN PAUL II

The Fundamental Rights of Man

Address to the President and Other Government Officials, Brasilia, Brazil June 30, 1980

MAY MY FIRST WORD TO YOU be to express my profound gratitude to Your Excellency. And I want to express this gratitude using one of the first expressions I learned in my recent study of the Portuguese language and which has a special meaning for me: *Muito obrigado* (many thanks). Many thanks for the generous welcome affirmed and demonstrated since Your Excellency became aware of my intention to accede to the wishes of my brother bishops of Brazil that I visit this country.

Many thanks for the kind presence of Your Excellency at the airport at the moment when I stepped on Brazilian soil and for the kind words you have just spoken to me. I ask that you consider them directed not just to me, but to the mission which has been vested in me and in the universal Church of which I am pastor.

The trips I am taking, following the initiative of my predecessors, above all Paul VI, constitute a very important aspect to me of my pontifical ministry and of the pastoral governance of the Church. They have a specific apostolic character and strictly pastoral objective, but in addition to this religious character, they carry also a message specifically about man, his values, his dignity, and his social life.

I come, therefore, to meet with the Church of Brazil, with the

---

Reprinted from "Origins" (published by the National Catholic News Service), July 17, 1980.

Catholic community that constitutes the great majority of the population of this vast and populous nation. But I also come wishing to meet with all the beloved people of Brazil.

Thus, this meeting is with almost half a millennium of human and religious history. In this history there is certainly the inevitable lightness-darkness that is found in the history of every people. May God give his help so that light always prevails over the shadows. In the historical profile of this illustrious nation, I want to emphasize three points:

—The well-known Brazilian ecumenism, which has been capable of integrating peoples and values of diverse ethnic backgrounds, which surely contributed to the characteristics of openness and universality of the culture of this country.

—Evangelization, which was done in such a way and with such continuance that it left profound marks on the lives of this people, providing without doubt, to the degree to which this fits in the mission of the Church, principles, norms, and moral and spiritual energies which shaped the human and national community.

—The youthful energy of the population, with its respective traditions and diverse qualities, surely guarantees that the nation will overcome the obstacles that will be found in its historic course, leading to a better tomorrow.

Evangelized from the beginning, the Brazilian people have lived the faith and the message of Christ, certainly not without problems, but with a sincerity and simplicity clearly attested to by its traditions, in which can be seen glimpses of options, interior attitudes, and behavior in fact Christian.

In addition, as Your Excellency had the kindness to mention, there are many ties that link Brazil to the Apostolic See in Rome, distinguishing a century and a half of friendly official relations, uninterrupted and ever more solid with the passage of time. They have a guarantee of authenticity in the love and devotion of the Brazilians to the vicar of Christ. The warmth of the reception which is given me here is an expression of this.

Mr. President, honorable members of the Congress, the Senate, the Supreme Court, the ministers of state, ladies and gentlemen: With your honorable presence here on my arrival and now in this meeting you wanted to honor the pastor of the universal Church, an honor for which he is extremely appreciative: *Muito obrigado* once again to each one of you personally.

I want to take this opportunity to express the highest esteem for the noble mission you carry out. The mandate you have received confers on you the privilege—that is also an obligation—to serve the common good of the whole nation, serving the Brazilian people. May God help you always to fulfill this mandate.

In my apostolic pilgrimages throughout the world I also want, with the help of God, to be the bearer of a message and collaborate in the humble but indispensable way which is my role so that an authentic meaning of man prevails in the world, not confined in strict anthropocentrism, but open to God.

I have a vision of man that has no fear in saying: Man cannot abdicate from himself nor from the place to which he belongs in the visible world. Man cannot become a slave to things, to material riches, to consumerism, to economic systems, or to that which he himself produces. Man cannot be made a slave to anyone or to anything.

Man cannot eliminate the transcendent—in the last analysis, God—without cutting himself off from his total being. Man in the end will only be able to find light for his own "mystery" in the mystery of Christ.

How beneficial would it be for the world if there were an understanding of man from his truth, as the only one capable of giving a human dimension to the diverse initiatives of daily life—political, economic, social, cultural, and the like. Rapidly this would become a base for programs of the "true civilization," which can only be a "civilization of love."

Attending to its proper mission and with clear respect for the legitimate institutions of the temporal order, the Church can only be pleased with all that is honest, just, and valid which exists in those institutions for the service of man. It can only see with satisfaction the efforts to save and promote the fundamental rights and liberties of all human persons and ensure these responsible participation in the social and community life.

For this very reason the Church does not cease to proclaim the reforms needed for the safety and promotion of those values without which no society worthy of the name can prosper, that is, reforms aimed at a more just society and which are in accord with the dignity of the human being.

Thus, it urges those responsible for the common good, particularly those who call themselves Christians, to undertake in a timely way, with decision and courage, with prudence and efficiency, those reforms which are based on Christian criteria and principles, objective justice, and an authentic social ethic.

Thus promoting such reforms is also a way of avoiding their being looked upon as just impulsive, in which no hesitation is made in using violence and the direct or indirect suppression of the rights and fundamental, inseparable liberties of the dignity of man.

Wishing the dear Brazilian people an always growing fraternity based on an authentic sense of man, with liberty, equality, respect, generosity, and love among all its members, and with a lucid and solid opening for humanity and for the world, I wish you a safe and secure peace, based on mutal work and the striving of all for progress and well-being.

I wish you also the sufficient and indispensable goods for the development of the human person. I ask God that each Brazilian of birth or adoption respect and always see respected the fundamental rights of all peoples. To proclaim and defend these rights, without setting them before the rights of God or silencing the obligations that correspond to them, is a constant of the life of the Church in virtue of the Gospels which are entrusted to it.

Thus, do not cease to invite all men of good will and encourage their children to the respect and cultivation of these rights—the right to life, to security, to work, to a home, to health, to education, to religious expression, both private and public, to participation, and the like.

Among these rights it is impossible not to mention as a priority the right of parents to have children as they wish, receiving at the same time what is needed to educate them in dignity, and the right of bearing life.

We know how many of these rights are being threatened in our days in the whole world.

I heartily bless what is done here in communion with universal efforts, which can only be for the benefit of the poorest and most marginalized persons afflicted by the undeserved frustrations of which they are victims.

In this sense, it is never too late to remember that never has a transformation of political, social, or economic structures been consolidated, if not followed by a sincere "conversion" of the mind, the will, and the heart of man, with all its truth.

This has to happen, taking into account, on the one hand, the avoidance of pernicious confusions between liberty and instinct, of self-interest, of fighting, or of domination, and, on the other hand, the creation of solidarity and fraternal love which are immune to any false autonomy in relation to God.

In this line of thinking, all of society is co-responsible. But initiatives and the human direction and logic of the processes depend in large part on those who are invested with positions of government and of leadership.

It depends on its original task of renewing and forming attitudes with adequate, constant, and patient processes of education and of utilizing good will, always enlightened by the "certainty that it is" man, the final beneficiary of his responsibilities and worries, as you wrote to me a while ago, Your Excellency.

The particular qualities of the Brazilian people, united with your long Christian tradition, will bring you to respond with certainty to the call and the challenge of the third millennium which approaches and the communion of minds and hearts in the search for the common good.

Clarified, proposed, and generated by the leaders, and with corresponding free, educated, and joint participation of all, you must continue to serve man and the supreme good of peace in this great nation, in this continent, and in the world.

Reiterating my gratitude to your excellencies for the reception and all the attention, I ardently wish for God's abundant blessings on Brazil through the intercession of Our Lady of Aparecida, your patron saint.

JOHN PAUL II

Poverty, Abundance, and Compassion

Address in Vidigal, Rio de Janeiro, Brazil July 2, 1980

1. WHEN JESUS CLIMBED the mountain and began to proclaim the teachings we all know as the Sermon on the Mount to all the people about him, the beatitudes flowed from his lips before anything else. The first of them proclaims: "Blessed are the poor in spirit, because theirs is the kingdom of God" (Matt. 5:3).

There is only one mountain in Galilee where Christ uttered his beatitudes. However there are so many places all over the world where the same are announced and heard.

Many are the hearts that do not cease reflecting on the meaning of those words said once and for all. They do not cease meditating on them. Their only wish is to practice them with all their heart. They try to live these beatitudes in their truth.

On Brazilian soil there are certainly many places like that. And here there were and are many, many of these hearts.

When I thought about how I should present myself to the inhabitants of this country which I am visiting for the first time, I felt it my duty to present myself above all through the teaching of the eight beatitudes. I felt the wish to talk about these to you, people of Vidigal.

Through you I also would like to talk to all who in Brazil live in the same conditions. Blessed are the poor in spirit.

Reprinted from "Origins" (published by the National Catholic News Service), July 17, 1980.

2. Among you are many poor. The Church in the Brazilian land wants to be the Church of the poor. She wishes that in this great country the first beatitude of the Sermon on the Mount may be fulfilled.

The poor in spirit are the ones who are more open to God and to "God's wonders" (Acts 2:11). They are poor because they are always ready to accept this gift from heaven which comes from God. They are poor in spirit, those who live knowing that they have received all from God's hands as a free gift and who appreciate everything they receive.

They are constantly thankful, they unceasingly repeat: "All is grace, thank our Lord God." At the same time, Jesus says of them that they are "pure of heart," "meek."

They are those who "hunger and thirst for justice." They are frequently "the afflicted." They are those who are "peacemakers" and "persecuted for justice's sake."

They are, finally, the "merciful" (cf. Matt. 5:3-10). In fact the poor, the poor in spirit, are more merciful. For that reason hearts open to God are more open to men. They are ready to help and to be useful. They are ready to share what they own. They are ready to welcome a widow or an abandoned orphan.

They always find one more place in the midst of the limitations they live in. And even so they always find some food, a piece of bread on their poor table.

Poor, but generous. Poor, but magnanimous. I know there are a lot of people like that among you here, to whom I am addressing my words, and in other parts of Brazil as well.

3. Do Christ's words about the poor in spirit perhaps make one forget about injustices? Do they allow us to leave unsolved the problems raised by the whole of the so-called social problem?

Problems that remain in human history assume different forms at different moments of history, and their intensity depends on the dimension of each society in particular as well as the proportion of continents, the whole world in a word. It is natural that these problems assume their own dimension in this land, a Brazilian dimension.

Christ's words calling the "poor in spirit" happy do not claim to suppress all these problems. On the contrary, they make them more evident, focusing them upon this most essential point, man, the human heart, every man without exception, man in regard to God and at the same time in regard to other men.

Does not being poor in spirit precisely make a man more open toward others, that is, toward God and his fellow man?

Is it not true that this beatitude of the "poor in spirit" also contains a warning and an accusation?

Is it not true that it tells the ones who are not "poor in spirit" that they are out of God's kingdom and that the kingdom of God is not and never will be shared by them? Thinking of these "rich" men who are closed to God and to mankind, without mercy, did not Christ say in another passage, "Woe to you" (Luke 6:24)?

"Woe to you." These words sound severe and threatening, especially in the mouth of Christ, who always spoke kindly and gently and who used to repeat, "May God bless you." However, he will also say, "Woe to you."

4. All over the world the Church wants to be the Church of the poor. The Church in Brazil also wants to be the Church of the poor, that is, she wants to draw out all the truth in Christ's beatitudes and especially this first one: "Blessed are the poor in spirit." She wants to teach this truth and practice it, as Christ came to do and to teach.

The Church also wants to draw out all that in the teaching of the eight beatitudes refers to each man: the poor, the one who lives in penury; the one who lives in abundance and well-being; and, finally, the one who has an excess and has more than he needs. The same truths of the first beatitude refer to each one in a different way.

The Church tells the poor, the ones who live in misery, that they are particularly close to God and his kingdom, but at the same time she tells them that it is not permissible for them and their families—for anyone—to be reduced arbitrarily to misery.

It is necessary to do everything licit to assure oneself and one's family whatever is necessary for life and maintenance. In poverty it is above all necessary to keep human dignity and also that magnanimity, that openness of heart toward others, that readiness which precisely distinguishes the poor, the poor in spirit.

To those who live in abundance or at least with a certain well-being, for which they have the necessities (even though they may not save), the Church who wishes to be the Church of the poor says: "Enjoy the results of your work and of rightful industry, but in the name of Christ's words, in the name of human brotherhood and of social solidarity, do not stay closed in yourselves.

"Think about the poor. Think about the ones who do not have what is needed, the ones who live in chronic want, who suffer hunger. Share with them. Share in an organized and methodical way."

May abundance never deprive you of the spiritual fruits of the Sermon on the Mount or separate you from the beatitudes of the poor in spirit.

And the Church of the poor says the same, with greater force, to those who have an excess, who live in abundance, who live in luxury. She tells them: "Look around you a bit. Does it not hurt your heart? Do you not feel the stings of your conscience for your surplus and abundance? If not, if you only want to 'get' more and more, if your model is profit and pleasure, remember that man's value is measured not by what he owns but by what he 'is.' "

So someone who has saved much and thinks that everything in life is reduced to that should remember that he might be worth much less than some of those poor people, that in his soul and in God's eyes maybe he is "much less of a man" than they.

The measure of wealth, money, and luxury is not the same as the measure of the real dignity of men.

So those who have a superabundance should avoid closing in on themselves in attachment to their riches, a spiritual blindness. May they avoid this with all their strength. May all the gospel truth be with them, especially the meaning of these words: "Blessed are the poor in spirit because theirs is the kingdom of heaven" (Matt. 5:3).

May this truth upset them.

May it be a continuous warning and challenge to them.

May it never allow them for even one minute to become blinded by selfishness and the satisfaction of their own desires.

If you have a lot, if you have a great deal, remember that you must give a lot, that there is much to give. And you should think how to give, how to organize all socio-economic life and each of its sectors so that this life will tend toward equality among men and not toward an abyss among them.

If you know much and you are of high social rank, do not even for one minute forget that the higher you are, the more you should serve. Serve others.

Otherwise you will find yourselves in danger of keeping yourselves and your lives from the field of the beatitudes and in particular from the first one: "Blessed are the poor in spirit."

The "rich" who, by means of their wealth, do not stop from "giving themselves" and "serving others" are "poor in spirit" as well.

So the Church of the poor speaks first and above all of man. To each man and so to all men. She is the universal Church, the Church of the mystery of the incarnation, not the church of one single class or one single race.

She speaks in the name of her own truth. This truth is realistic. We should take into consideration each human reality, each injustice, each tension, each conflict. The Church of the poor will not serve anything that causes tensions and makes strife among men explode.

The only fight, the only one that the Church will serve, is the noble one for truth and justice, the one for the real good, the one where the Church is at one with each man.

On this road the Church fights with the "sword of truth," without abstaining from encouraging as well as warning, sometimes in a very severe way (as Christ did). Very often she even threatens and shows the consequences of hypocrisy and evil.

In this evangelical fight the Church of the poor will not serve immediate political purposes or power struggles. She tries at the same time with great care to ensure that her words and actions are not used for that purpose, that is, "instrumentalized."

The Church of the poor speaks to "mankind," to each and to all men. At the same time she speaks to society as a whole and to different social levels, to different groups and professions. She speaks to systems and to social structures, both socio-economic and socio-political.

She speaks the language of the Gospel, explaining it in light of human knowledge but without introducing strange, heterodox elements contrary to her spirit. She speaks to everybody in the name of Christ, as well as in the name of man, particularly to those for whom Christ's name is not everything, does not express all the truth about man that this name contains.

So the Church of the poor speaks like this: You, particularly the ones who have power in decision-making, you, on whom the world situation depends, do everything so that the life of each man in your country may become "more human," more worthy of man.

Do everything so that at least gradually the abyss that divides the few "excessively rich" from the great multitudes of poor, those who live in want, may disappear.

Do everything so that this abyss will not grow but shrink and tend toward social equality, so that the unjust distribution of goods will give way to a more just distribution.

Do it out of consideration for each man who is your fellow man and your fellow citizen. Do it out of consideration for the common good of all. Do it for yourself. Only a socially just society, one that strives to be ever more just, has a reason to exist. Only such a society has a future ahead of it.

A society that is not socially just and that does not try to become so has its future in danger. Think, then, about the past and look at it nowadays and plan a better future for your whole society.

All this is included in what Christ said in his Sermon on the Mount, in the context of this single sentence: "Blessed are the poor in spirit, because theirs is the kingdom of heaven."

Dear brothers and sisters, with this message I renew my feelings of deep affection, and as a pledge of God's blessing for you and your families, I give you my apostolic blessing.

JOHN PAUL II

Politics Must Serve the Common Good

Address to Workers, São Paulo, Brazil July 3, 1980

1. I FEEL HAPPY AND HONORED to be here among you today in São Paulo. I am happy to discover your city, this immense metropolis of incredible industrial development. Incredible industrial growth goes hand in hand here with accelerating urbanization, which is at once fascinating and worrying.

I am happy chiefly because I am discovering this city through persons, through you, men and women, who work, suffer, and hope here. You came here from all corners of this immense country and from the whole world. You came so as to earn your living and to collaborate in a great common task which is vital for the whole nation: the construction of a city worthy of human beings.

Yes, because São Paulo is you. São Paulo is not mainly these material achievements. They are not always guided by a just and full sense of man and society, nor are they always suitable for organizing an environment where it may be possible to live lives worthy of human beings. São Paulo is also the very many people on the fringes of society, the unemployed, the underemployed, or the ill employed, who do not find ways of using their hands and developing properly their generous resources of mind and heart.

São Paulo is you. You are gathered here to celebrate your dignity as workers and manifest your readiness to work together to build a city to the measure of your hopes as humans. São Paulo is you, assembled here to seek in the Gospel of Jesus Christ the light

Reprinted from "Origins" (published by the National Catholic News Service), July 17, 1980.

and energy necessary for achieving the task that awaits you, that of turning São Paulo into a fully human city.

2. Yes, Jesus Christ, the Lord of the universe and of history, brings us together here today. The Pope visits you in his name today. Workers, my brothers and sisters, I give thanks to God for having allowed me to be among you. I thank you for the deep joy that this meeting is causing this minister of Jesus Christ. In the days of his youth, in his native Poland, he knew directly the condition of being a manual worker. He knew its greatness and harshness, its hours of joyfulness and its moments of anguish, the accomplishments and frustrations that go with this condition of life. From the bottom of my heart I say to you what the apostle St. Paul said to the Romans, "I long to see you and to share with you some spiritual gift to strengthen you; rather, what I wish is that we may be mutually encouraged by our common faith" (Rom. 1:11-12).

Therefore, I invite you, Christian workers, my brothers and sisters, to begin to celebrate in joyfulness and friendship what Jesus offers to one and all of us: the faith, hope, and charity with which Jesus enlivens our hearts when we meet in his name, in his Church, which he established for gathering up his gifts and distributing them to all. Christian festivity gives joy. It is not a luxury reserved for the rich. The whole world is invited to take part. Last year those on the fringes of society in another big metropolis, New York, sang the "Alleluia" of resurrection with me. And not long ago Africa, the Africa of poverty, gave the Pope and the world the spectacle of an unforgettable festivity.

And this festivity arises from the conviction that we are loved by God and that God is with us. God is visiting us. The kingdom of God is among us. This is the inexhaustible source of our joyfulness: We know how God loves us and recognizes us, we know that we are free from sin, that we have been raised to the insuperable dignity of being God's children, rich in faith, hope, and love, which the Holy Spirit pours out into our hearts. So let us celebrate our God and our Father, Jesus Christ our Lord and our brother, who brings us together.

The assembly of bishops at Puebla willed to commit the Church in Latin America to an option for the poor. That option is essentially this: that the poor have the Gospel preached to them, that the Church once again set all her energies to work so that Jesus Christ may be announced to all, chiefly the poor, and that all have access to this living fount, the table of the word and of bread, the sacraments, the community of the baptized. Here is the meaning of our meeting today, of our Christian feast. We shall go away from here to our tasks as citizens and workers with fresh enthusiasm. We shall go with a clearer consciousness of our dignity, of our rights, of our responsibilities. We shall go with renewed faith in the prodigious resources with which, by creating us in his image and likeness, he enriches us for being able to face the challenges of our time, the challenges of this metropolis that is São Paulo.

3. I speak to you in the name of Christ, in the name of the Church, the entire Church. It is Christ who sends his Church to all men and all societies with a message of salvation. This mission of the Church is carried out in view of two perspectives at once. There is the eschatological perspective. This regards man as a being whose final destination is God. There is the historical perspective. This looks at this same man in his concrete situation as incarnated in the world of today. This message of salvation is brought by the Church in virtue of her mission to every man, to the family, to the various social environments, to nations, and to the whole of mankind. It is a message of love and fraternity, a message of justice and solidarity. It is in the first place meant for the most needy. In a word, it is a message of peace and a just social order.

I will repeat here before you what I said to the workers of St. Denis, a workers' quarter in another big city, Paris. I began with those most profound words of the Magnificat. I chose to consider together with them that "the world designed by God is a world of justice; that the order which ought to regulate relations among men is based on justice; that this order ought to be unceasingly realized in this world, and even that it must always be realized anew, as the situations and social systems increase and develop, as new economic conditions and possibilities, new technical and productive possibilities, and at the same time, new possibilities and needs in the distribution of goods arise" (Homily at St. Denis, May 31, 1980).

When the Church proclaims the Gospel, it also tries, without abandoning its specific role of evangelization, to make sure all aspects of social life wherein justice is manifested undergo a transformation toward justice. The common good of society demands as a fundamental requirement that society be just. Persisting injustice, the lack of justice, threatens society's existence from both inside and outside in the same way as everything that represents an attack upon its sovereignty or seeks to impose ideologies or models upon it, and all economic and political blackmail, all use of the force of arms, can threaten society from outside and inside.

This threat from the interior really exists when trust is placed solely in the economic laws of growth and greater profit for regulating the domain of the distribution of goods, when the results of progress touch vast sectors of the population only marginally or not at all.

The danger exists also inasmuch as a deep abyss exists between a very large minority of rich on the one side and on the other side a majority of people living in want and penury.

4. The common good of society will ever be the new name of justice. It cannot be obtained through violence, because violence destroys what it seeks to create. It does this both when it is used to maintain the privileges of some and when it is used in an attempt to impose necessary transformations. The changes demanded for there to be a just social order ought to be achieved through constant action along the path of peaceful reforms. Such action should always be effective, although often gradual and progressive.

This is the duty of all. It is particularly the duty of those who hold power in society, whether economic power or political power. All power finds its justification only in the common good, in achieving a just social order. Consequently, power should never serve to protect the interests of one group to the detriment of the others. The class struggle is not the path leading to a just social order, because it bears in it the risk of raising the unfavored up to becoming the privileged, thereby creating a fresh situation of injustice against those who have so far had advantages. One cannot build with hatred or the destruction of others.

Rejecting the class struggle means opting resolutely for a noble struggle in favor of social justice. The various power centers and the various representatives of society ought to be able to meet, to coordinate their efforts and come to agreement on clear and efficacious programs. This is what the Christian formula for creating a just society consists in. The whole of society ought to be at one with all people and in the first place with those who need help, the poor. The option for the poor is a Christian option; it is also the option of a society that is concerned with the true common good.

5. Let us listen to what Christ himself said in this regard. He was talking to the multitude that had come from all over the region and from beyond the frontiers to see him. He was seated among his disciples. He began his discourse with these words, "How blessed are the poor in spirit; the kingdom of God is theirs" (Matt. 5:3). He addressed those words to others besides those who were listening; he addressed them to us too, gathered here in São Paulo in Brazil. Twenty centuries have taken nothing from the impelling importance, the gravity and the hope contained in those words of the Lord. "How blessed are the poor in spirit!" These words are valid for each of us. This invitation is a call to each of us. What Christ asks from all is that they acquire the spirit of being poor.

Those who have possessions ought to acquire the spirit of being poor. They ought to open their hearts to the poor, for if they do not do so, situations of injustice will not change. The political structure or social system can be changed, but a just and stable social order will not be achieved without change of heart and conscience. Those who have no possessions, those who are in need, should also acquire "the spirit of being poor"; they should not permit material poverty to take their human dignity from them, for this dignity is more important than all goods.

It is in this connection that the Christian doctrine on man gives singular value to human labor. This teaching has been nourished on the Gospel, on the Bible, and by centuries of experience. The dignity of labor. The nobility of labor. You know the dignity and nobility of your labor as you work in order to live, in order to live better, so as to win your families' daily bread. You feel wounded in your affections as fathers and mothers at seeing your children ill nourished, you who are so content and proud when you can offer them a loaded table, when you can clothe them well, give them a decent, cozy home, give them schooling and education in hopes of a better future. Your labor is a service, a service to your families and to the whole city. It is a service in which man himself grows to the degree that he gives himself for others. Work is a discipline wherein the personality is strengthened.

Your prime and fundamental aspiration is therefore to be able to work. What sufferings, what anxieties and miseries are caused by unemployment! Therefore, the prime and fundamental preoccupation of all, of those in government, politicians, labor-union leaders, and owners of enterprises, ought to be to give work to all. It is not realistic, hence it is not admissible, to expect to find a solution to the crucial problem of employment as a more or less automatic result of an order of things and economic development, of whatever kind, where employment is seen as only a secondary effect. Both the theory and the practice of economics ought to have the courage to consider employment and its modern possibilities as a central element in its objectives.

6. It is a matter of justice that working conditions be as worthy as possible, that social insurance be perfected so as to permit all to face social risks, hardships, and burdens on the basis of increasing social solidarity. It is legitimate to demand that wages be adjusted in their diverse and complementary forms to the point where it will be possible to say that the worker really and equitably shares in the wealth that he has contributed to creating through his solidarity and his integral participation in the enterprise, the profession, and the national economy concerned.

The Church has never stopped developing a very rich doctrine on all these points, mainly since the first great social encyclical *Rerum Novarum*. I call upon you all, workers and those with responsible positions in politics, the professions, and labor unions, to give fresh attention to this teaching. No one is going to find ready-made solutions, but clarification and stimuli for thought and practice may be found there. The task is delicate. This complex

mass of problems contains many factors—employment, invest-
ment, wages—that react with each other. It cannot be settled
through demagogy, through ideological enchantments, or through
cold and theoretical scientism, which, contrary to the true scientific
spirit, would leave verification of its suppositions to an uncertain
future.

I will once more repeat here what I said in regard to employment: To expect that the solution to the problems of pay, social
insurance, and work conditions will flow naturally from a kind of
automatic extension of a certain economic order is not realistic,
and therefore is not admissible. The economy will be viable only if
it is human, for man and through man.

7. For this same reason it is very important for all actors in
economic life to have the practical possibility of taking part freely
and actively in working out and supervising decisions regarding
themselves at all levels. Pope Leo XIII already affirmed in *Rerum
Novarum* the right of workers to meet in free associations for the
purpose of making their voice heard, defending their interests, and
contributing in a responsible manner to the common good. The
demands and the discipline required by the common good apply to
all within the framework of laws and contracts that can always be
improved.

The Church proclaims and sustains these various rights of workers because men and their dignity are at stake. It does this in the
deep and ardent conviction that a man who works becomes a
cooperator with God. He is made in God's image. He has received
the mission of administering the universe so as to develop its riches
and assure them a universal destination, to unite men in mutual
service and in common creation of a worthy and beautiful way of
living for the glory of the Creator.

Workers, never forget the great nobility which, as men and
women and as Christians, you ought to imprint upon your work,
even the most humble and insignificant. Never let yourselves be
degraded by work. Rather seek to live thoroughly that true dignity
of labor which God's word and the Church's teaching put in evidence. Work really makes you above all collaborators with God in

carrying forward the work of his creation. Go on with that dynamism which is contained in the command given to the first man to populate the earth and rule it (cf. Gen. 1:28). Go on, with sweat on your brows, yes, but above all with just pride in being created in the image of God himself.

Work associates you more closely with the redemption that Christ accomplished through the cross. It does so when it leads you to accept everything that is painful, fatiguing, mortifying, and crucifying in the daily monotony; when it leads you even to unite your sufferings with the Saviour's sufferings so as to fill up "what is lacking in the sufferings of Christ, for the sake of his body, the church" (Col. 1:24). Therefore, work leads you in the end to feel at one with all your brethren here in Brazil and in the whole world. It makes you builders of the great human family and of the whole Church as well in the bond of charity, for each is called to aid the other (cf. Gal. 6:2) in ever recurrent need for mutual collaboration and in that interpersonal aid whereby we men and women are necessary to each other, without excluding anyone.

This is the Christian concept of labor. It sets out from faith in God the creator and, through Christ the redeemer, arrives at the edification of human society, oneness with man. Without this vision any effort is lacking and wasted, however tenacious it may be. It is fated to disappoint, to fail. Build on this foundation. And if they tell you that in order to defend labor's gains it is necessary to put this Christian vision of existence aside or even to cancel it out, do not believe them. Without God and without Christ man builds on sand. He betrays his own origin and his nobility. In the end he comes to do harm to man, to offend his brother.

8. You work in the setting of a big city that continues to grow rapidly. It is a reflection of the incredible possibilities of the human race, which is capable of admirable achievements but is also capable of tearing and grinding man down when spiritual motivation and moral orientation are absent.

An exclusivist economic logic often invades all fields of existence, spoiling the environment, threatening families, and destroying all respect for the human person. Such logic is even more depraved by crass materialism. Factories discharge their waste, deform and pollute the environment; the air becomes unbreathable. Waves of migrants pile up in indecent shacks; many lose hope there and end in misery. Children, youngsters, adolescents, find no living space for developing their physical and mental energies fully. They are often restricted to unhealthful quarters or must wander in the streets and live in the flow of traffic between cement walls and the faceless multitude that wears them down and never becomes individually known to them.

There are districts where life is lived with all modern comforts. Besides them are others where the most elementary things are not to be found. Some peripheral areas are growing in disorder. Development is often a gigantic version of the parable of the rich man and Lazarus. The proximity between luxury and penury heightens the feeling of frustration in the unfortunate. A fundamental question therefore becomes imperative: How is the city to be transformed into a truly human city in its natural environment, its constructions, and its institutions?

An essential condition is that of giving the economy human meaning and logic. What I said about work holds good here too. It is necessary to liberate the various fields of existence from the dominion of subjugating economism. It is necessary to put economic demands in their proper place and create a multiform social texture that will avoid massification. No one is dispensed from cooperating in this task. We can all do something in ourselves and around ourselves. Is it not true that the most neglected districts are often the places where solidarity arouses gestures of the greatest self-detachment and generosity? Christians, wherever you may be, take your share of responsibility in this immense effort for bringing human restructuring to the city. Faith makes this a duty. Faith and experience together will give you light and energy to start moving.

9. Christians have the right and the duty to contribute so far as they are able to building up society. And they do so through associational and institutional frameworks that a free society operates with participation by all. The Church as such does not claim to run society or to take the place of lawful organs of deliberation and action. It only claims to serve all those who at any level take on responsibilities for the common good. Its service is essentially in the ethical and religious order. but, in accordance with its mission and in order to guarantee such service, the Church demands with full right a space for the indispensable liberty to seek to maintain its specific religious nature.

So all communities of Christians, both basic communities and parishes, diocesan communities, or the whole national church community, ought to make their specific contributions to building up society. All man's concerns must be taken into consideration. This is so because evangelization, the Church's reason for being, any ecclesial community's reason for being, would not be complete unless it took into account the relations existing between the gospel message and man's personal and social living, between the commandment to love one's suffering and needy neighbor, and concrete situations where injustice must be combated and justice and peace installed.

May this meeting of ours today around Jesus Christ bring with it the certainty that the Church wills to be present with all its gospel message in the heart of the city, in the heart of the poorest people of the city, in the heart of each one of you. You are loved by God, workers of São Paulo and Brazil. And you ought to love God. This is the secret of your joy, of a joy that will flow from your hearts and shine in your faces and on the city's face as a sign that it is a human city.

JOHN PAUL II

Peaceful Reform vs. Violent Revolution

Address in Salvador, Brazil
July 6, 1980

DEAREST BROTHERS AND SISTERS,

1. Here I am in your city, which hangs, magnificent, over the Bay of All Saints. It is with immense joy that I contemplate you gathered in this numerous assembly at this stadium.

I greet your cardinal, Avelar Brandao Vilela, his coadjutor archbishop, his auxiliary bishop, and his closest collaborators. I greet the state and city authorities. I greet the priests and men and women religious here present. I greet this multitude, in which I see very dear sons and daughters. I search your faces one by one, I grasp your hands and offer you an embrace. In the Church we are not a shapeless and faceless mass, we are not impersonal and unknown, one to the other. We are the people of God. We are loved, one by one, by the Father, in the Son, through the Holy Spirit. We are persons capable of responding to the appeal of this God's everlasting love. He has known us always and predestined us to conformity with the image of his Son. He called us, he justified us, and he glorified us (cf. Rom. 8:30). So, we are brethren, we love each other and form one single body.

I salute you, people of God who are in São Salvador da Bahia. I greet this church, which is eternally loved by the Lord, I greet it with the words used by St. Paul, which the liturgy makes its own: "The grace of our Lord Jesus Christ, the love of the Father and the communion of the Holy Spirit be with you all" (cf. 2 Cor. 13:13).

Reprinted from "Origins" (published by the National Catholic News Service), July 31, 1980.

2. This meeting is dedicated to "The Builders of a Pluralistic Society Today." They have come here especially, as a sign of the extraordinarily rich reality of human, intellectual, and social powers which Brazil represents in the world. I therefore greet you in a particular fashion, brothers and sisters. You make construction of society your ideal, your honor, your daily work.

Every man is a builder of the society in which he lives. The Second Vatican Council brought out this truth: "The laity," it said, "must take on renewal of the temporal order as their own special obligation. Led by the light of the Gospel and the mind of the Church, and motivated by Christian love, let them act directly and definitively in the temporal sphere. As citizens they must cooperate with other citizens, using their own particular skills and acting on their own responsibility. Everywhere and in all things they must seek the justice characteristic of God's kingdom" (Decree on the Apostolate of the Laity, 7).

In all of you I see the builders of the Brazil of today and tomorrow. If Brazil has arrived within sight of the twenty-first century as a nation full of promise, it is thanks to the efforts of individuals who have contributed toward building up their own community, their city, and their nation by seeking their own improvement and the well-being due them, their families, and their fellow citizens. You are likewise called to construct the future of your country, a future of peace, prosperity, and concord. That future will be guaranteed only when all citizens, in accordance with their responsibilities and with a single common concern, will be able to create and maintain social relations based on respect for the common good that puts man, God's creation, in the center.

I would vigorously emphasize this reality. I address one and all of you, those present and those absent: workers and industrialists, professional men and women and students, economists and artists, men of science and technology, artisans, craftsmen, journalists, politicians and people on the land, dwellers in big and small cities. All of you in some way and to some degree are builders of the pluralist society of today.

The word *pluralist* itself already tells of the complexity and richness of the modern world, its dynamism, its vitality, its continuous ascent toward higher levels. Congratulations, men and women who are building the world of today and of tomorrow.

3. What course is the world on? Where is it going? I am not speaking to you here as an economist or sociologist, but by virtue of my mandate and mission as universal pastor of that church which my unforgettable predecessor Paul VI described as "expert in humanity."

The grand spectacle of power and creative and constructive capacity in man which modern society displays arouses amazement and admiration in us. No less frightening is the spectacle of alienation to which society has very often been reduced. When I first came to your continent I felt the need to say to the bishops of Latin America assembled at Puebla: "One of the most notable weaknesses of present civilization lies in an inadequate vision of man. Ours is doubtless the epoch in which there has been most writing and talking about man, it is the epoch of humanisms and anthropocentrisms. Yet, paradoxically, it is also the epoch of profound anxieties in man about his identity and destiny, and of abasement of man to levels once unimaginable. It is the epoch when human values are trampled down as never before" (Opening Address, I, 9).

There is no need to tell you, for you all know very well, of the harm done to man by a self-sufficient culture and technology closed to the transcendent, man reduced to being a sheer instrument of production, the victim of preconceived ideologies or the cold logic of economic laws, manipulated for utilitarian ends or group interests, that disregarded or disregard man's true good.

The very word *pluralism* bears a danger within it. In a society that likes to call itself *pluralist* there is actually a diversity of beliefs, of ideologies, of philosophical ideas. However, acknowledgment of this reality, this plurality, does not exempt me—nor any Christian adhering to the Gospel—from affirming what is the necessary base, the unquestionable principle that ought to support all activity directed toward constructing a society that ought to meet man's requirements, both on the level of material goods and on the level of spiritual and religious goods, a society founded on a system of values which can defend it from individual or collective egoism.

4. Conscious as I am of the universal mission that has brought me among you in these days, I have the duty to proclaim God's word loudly: "Unless the Lord build the house they labor in vain who build it" (Ps. 126:1).

This is the reply that the Church must give, today above all: Society may not be built without God, without God's help. That would be a contradiction. God is the guarantee of a society made to man's measure: First, because he imprinted the supreme nobility of his image and likeness within man (cf. Gen. 1:26 ff.); then, because Jesus Christ came to restore that image that had been stained by sin. As "redeemer of man," he gave it back the unrenounceable dignity of its origin. External structures, international communities, states, cities, each man's activity, ought to lay stress upon this reality and give it the space it needs. Otherwise they fall to pieces or become a facade without a soul.

The Church founded by Christ shows the man of today the path to follow for building up the earthly city, which is the prelude to the heavenly city, although it is not free of antipathies and contradictions. The Church shows the way to building society to function in terms of man, in respect for man. Its task is to bring the leaven of the Gospel into all fields of human activity. It is in Christ that the Church is "an expert in man."

Perusing the history of your fatherland, I could not fail to notice that as it carried out its mission in other centuries, the Church contributed to making that same history, to determining the values that constitute the cultural history of the Brazilian people. The Church is linked to your people in such a way that to eliminate it would mean mutilating the people's social and cultural patrimony. Therefore the Church must go on collaborating in the construction of your society, by discerning and nourishing the aspirations for justice and peace that it finds in individuals and in the people, with its wisdom and its effort to promote such aspirations. The Church will respect the competence of public authorities in these matters.

It will not claim to intervene in politics; it will not aspire to share in managing temporal affairs. Its specific contribution will be to fortify the spiritual and moral bases of society by doing what is possible for all or any activity in the field of the common good, carried out in harmony and coherence with the directives and demands of a human and Christian ethic.

5. Still with concrete reality as the object, the concrete task performed in common, this service is above all a service of formation of consciences. It means proclaiming the moral law and its demands, denouncing errors and attacks against the moral law and man's dignity, upon which that law is based; it means clarifying, convincing.

This is what I observed in the already mentioned speech at Puebla: "Particular care must be given to forming a social conscience at all levels and in all sectors. When injustices increase and when the distance between rich and poor painfully increases too, social doctrine ought to be a valuable instrument for training and action, in a creative form, open to wide fields of the Church's action" (Opening Address, III, 7).

The Church does not propose a concrete political or economic model in its social doctrine; but it shows the way, presents principles. And it does so by reason of its evangelizing mission, by reason of the evangelical message, which has man as its objective, in his eschatological dimension, but also in the concrete context of his historical situation today; it does so because it believes in man's dignity, as being created in God's image, in the dignity that is intrinsic to every man and every woman, and every child, whatever be the place that he occupies in society.

Every man has the right to expect that society will respect his human dignity and allow him to maintain a life in accord with that dignity. In the speech which I delivered before the Organization of American States last year, I set forth man as the sole criterion giving meaning and direction to all commitment by those responsible for the common good, whether simple citizens or vested with power.

I proposed the concrete man as the criterion, in these words:

"When there is talk of the right to life, to physical and moral integrity, to nourishment, to shelter, to education, to health, to work, to responsible participation in the nation's life, the talk is of the human person. And this human person often happens to be in danger, famished, without a decent house and work, without access to the cultural heritage of his people or of mankind, and without voice enough to make his troubles heard. It is necessary to give fresh life to the great cause of all-around development. This ought to be done precisely by those who already enjoy those goods in one way or another. They ought to put themselves at the service of all those—so numerous on your continent—who are deprived of these same goods to a degree which is at times dramatic" (Speech to the OAS, October 6, 1979).

6. Putting man in the center of all social activity therefore means feeling concern at every injustice because it offends man's dignity. Taking man as the criterion means committing oneself to transformation of every unjust situation and reality, so as to turn them into elements for a just society.

That was the message which I directed to the authorities of this country; this is the meassage that I presented to the workers of São Paulo. This is also the message that I bring to you today, builders of society who are listening to me here in São Salvador da Bahia.

Every society ought to establish a just social order unless it wishes to be destroyed from within. This appeal is not a justification of the class struggle—for the class struggle is destined to sterility and destruction—but it is an appeal to a noble struggle for the sake of social justice throughout society.

All of you, who have taken the name of builders of society, have a certain power in your hands because of your positions, your situations, or your activities. Use that power in the service of social justice. Reject that kind of reasoning which is inspired by the collective egoism of a group or of a class or is based on the motivation of one-sided material profit. Reject violence as the means of resolving the problems of society, since violence is contrary to life, it destroys man. Apply your power, be it political, economic, or cultural, to the service of solidarity embracing the whole of man, in the first place men and women who are most in need, whose rights are most frequently violated. Put yourselves on the side of the poor in consistency with the Church's teaching, on the side of all who in some way are the most deprived of spiritual or material goods to which they have a right.

"How blessed are the poor in spirit" (Matt. 5:3). Blessed are they who know how to save their human dignity in the midst of want. But blessed also are they who do not let themselves be possessed by their possessions, who do not allow their sense of social justice to be stifled by attachment to their goods. Truly blessed are the poor in spirit!

7. In presenting this message of justice and love to you, the Church is true to its mission and aware of serving the good of society. It does not consider that it is its task to enter into political activities, but it knows that it is at the service of the good of mankind. The Church does not combat power, but proclaims that power is for the good of society and the safeguarding of society's sovereignty, that power is necessary. And that only this justifies it. The Church is convinced that it is its right and its duty to promote a social pastorate, that is, to exert an influence, through the means proper to it, so that society may become more just, thanks to joint, decided, but always peaceful action on the part of all citizens.

So I will speak to all who in some sector of society are builders of this society and to whom my word reaches, with the Church's word, here in Salvador or any other part of Brazil.

To you chiefly who have special responsibilities because of your position and power as Christians.

To you political leaders or militants I would remind you that the political act par excellence is that of being consistent with a moral calling and true to an ethical conscience which, above and beyond personal or group interests, has the common good of all citizens in view.

I speak to you, educators, who have the task of explaining to the young and holding a dialogue with them about the values through which they in their turn will become builders of society. I ask you to base your work on solid foundations and inculcate a sense of the dignity of the human person in our youth.

Entrepreneurs, traders, and industrialists, I exhort you to put man first in your plans and projects, that man who is a builder of society through his labor and the produce of his hands and his wits. He is first a builder of his own family, then of broader communities. Do not forget that every man has a right to work, not only in cities and in great industrial concentrations, but in the countryside as well.

Men of science, technicians, I have the right to remind you that the ethical always takes first place over the technical and man over things.

To you workers I have to say: Construction of society is not the task only of those who control the economy, industry, and agriculture. You also build society with your sweat, for your children and for the future. If you have the right to have your say about economic and industrial activity, you also have the duty to shape what you say according to the demands of the moral law, which is justice, dignity, and love.

For you specialists in communications I have a request: Do not shackle the soul of the masses with the power you hold, by sifting information and by promoting exclusively the consumer society, where abundance is accessible only to a minority. Be above all spokesmen for man, his rightful demands and his dignity. Be instruments of justice, of truth, and of love. Defend what is human, and give man access to full truth.

8. Yes, brothers and sisters, building society is first of all a matter of acquiring a conscience; not in the exclusive sense of gaining knowledge of the results of a certain situation analysis or survey of the evils of society, but in the full meaning of the word, that is, forming one's consciousness according to the demands of God's law, of Christ's message about man, of the ethical dimension of all human enterprise.

Building up society means committing oneself, taking the side of conscience, of the principles of justice, of brotherhood, of love, against the intentions of egoism, which spoils brotherhood, and hatred, which destroys.

Building society means going beyond barriers, divisions, oppositions, so as to work together. Man has the capacity to open to others. Christ asks us in a stunning way, "Who is my brother?" No lasting and truly human work is possible unless it is made for all, through collaboration by all vital forces in society, through interchange among all men and women without distinction of social position or economic situation.

Finally, building society means continual conversion of self, revision of one's attitudes, so as to detect sterile prejudices and discover one's own errors in order to open up to the imperatives of a conscience formed in the light of the dignity of every human person, as was revealed and confirmed by Jesus Christ. It means opening heart and spirit so that justice, love, and respect for man's dignity and destinies may penetrate thought and inspire action.

9. The Church, that "expert in mankind," offers its collaboration for building up a world to man's measure. But it also calls for your full, sincere, generous collaboration, without ulterior intentions.

It depends on each and every one of you whether the future of Brazil is to be a future of peace, whether Brazilian society is to be life together in justice. I believe that the time has come for every man and every woman in this immense country to resolve to use the wealth of their talents and consciences decidedly for giving life to the nation on a basis that will guarantee development of social realities and structures in justice. Anyone who reflects on the reality of Latin America, as it presents itself at this moment, is led to agree with the statement that the realization of justice on this continent faces a clear dilemma: Either it will come through profound and courageous reforms, according to principles that express the supremacy of the dignity of man, or it will come—but without lasting result and without benefit for man, of this I am convinced—through the forces of violence. Each one of you must feel that he is being challenged by this dilemma. Each one of you must make his choice at this historic hour.

Brothers and sisters, my friends, do not be afraid to look ahead, to go forward, to set off for the year 2000. A new world must arise. In God's name and man's, do not refuse. The Church expects much from you. "Will you, together with me, build the world, raise it, make it better and more worthy of you and your brethren, who are my brethren?" Do not frustrate Christ's expectation. Do not disappoint the hopes of man, your contemporary.

In this immense but stupendous effort, know that the Pope is with you, prays for you, has you in his heart, and, in Christ's name, blesses you.

A Note on the Appendixes

The texts of Appendixes A and B, excerpts from the Medellín Conclusions, are from *The Church in the Present-Day Transformation of Latin America in the Light of the Council,* published in 1973 by the United States Catholic Conference (USCC). The texts of Appendixes C, D, and E, excerpts from the Puebla Conclusions, are from *Evangelization at Present and in the Future of Latin America,* copyright 1979 by the National Conference of Catholic Bishops (NCCB). The offices of the USCC and the NCCB are at 1312 Massachusetts Avenue, N.W., Washington, D.C. 20005.

The following documents and addresses are cited by initial letters:

AO   Address to the Indians of Oaxaca and Chiapas, Oaxaca, Mexico, John Paul II, January 29, 1979

AWM   Address to Workers in Monterrey, Mexico, John Paul II, January 31, 1979

DH   *Dignitatis Humanae,* Declaration on Religious Freedom, Vatican II, 1965

EN   *Evangelii Nuntiandi,* Paul VI, 1975

GS   *Gaudium et Spes,* Pastoral Constitution on the Church in the Modern World, Vatican II, 1965

LG   *Lumen Gentium,* Dogmatic Constitution on the Church, Vatican II, 1964

Med-JU   Medellín Document on Justice, Second General Conference of Latin American Bishops, 1968

Med-OA   Medellín Opening Address, Second General Conference of Latin American Bishops, Paul VI, 1968

Med-PE   Medellín Document on Pastoral Concern for the Elites, Second General Conference of Latin American Bishops, 1968

Med-PR   Medellín Document on Priests, Second General Conference of Latin American Bishops, 1968

OA   *Octogesima Adveniens,* Paul VI, 1971

OAP   Opening Address at Puebla, Third General Conference of Latin American Bishops, John Paul II, 1979

PP   *Populorum Progressio,* Paul VI, 1967

PT   *Pacem in Terris,* John XXIII, 1963

RMS   Address to Religious Major Superiors, John Paul II, November 24, 1978

Justice

Latin American Bishops
Medellín, 1968

Second General Conference Statement, Chapter One

I. PERTINENT FACTS

1. There are in existence many studies of the Latin American people. The misery that besets large masses of human beings in all of our countries is described in all of these studies. That misery, as a collective fact, expresses itself as injustice which cries to the heavens (PP 30).

But what perhaps has not been sufficiently said is that in general the efforts which have been made have not been capable of assuring that justice be honored and realized in every sector of the respective national communities. Often families do not find concrete possibilities for the education of their children. The young demand their right to enter universities or centers of higher learning for both intellectual and technical training; the women, their right to a legitimate equality with men; the peasants, better conditions of life; or if they are workers, better prices and security in buying and selling; the growing middle class feels frustrated by the lack of expectations. There has begun an exodus of professionals and technicians to more developed countries; the small businessmen and industrialists are pressed by greater interests, and not a few large Latin American industrialists are gradually coming to be dependent on the international business enterprises. We cannot ignore the phenomenon of this almost universal frustration of legitimate aspirations which creates the climate of collective anguish in which we are already living.

2. The lack of socio-cultural integration, in the majority of our countries, has given rise to the superimposition of cultures. In the economic sphere, systems flourished which consider solely the potential of groups with great earning power. This lack of adaptation to the characteristics and to the potentials of all our people, in turn, gives rise to frequent political instability and the consolidation of purely formal institutions. To all of this must be added the lack of solidarity which, on the individual and social levels, leads to the committing of serious sins, evident in the unjust structures which characterize the Latin American situation.

II. DOCTRINAL BASES

3. The Latin American Church has a message for all men on this continent who "hunger and thirst after justice." The very God who creates men in his image and likeness, creates the "earth and all that is in it for the use of all men and all nations, in such a way that created goods can reach all in a more just manner" (GS 69), and gives them power to transform and perfect the world in solidarity (Gen. 1:26; GS 34). It is the same God who, in the fullness of time, sends his Son in the flesh, so that he might come to liberate all men from the slavery to which sin has subjected them (John 8:32-35): hunger, misery, oppression, and ignorance—in a word, that injustice and hatred which have their origin in human selfishness.

Thus, for our authentic liberation, all of us need a profound conversion so that "the kingdom of justice, love, and peace" might come to us. The origin of all disdain for mankind, of all injustice, should be sought in the internal imbalance of human liberty, which will always need to be rectified in history. The uniqueness of the Christian message does not so much consist in the affirmation of the necessity for structural change, as it does in the insistence on the conversion of men, which will in turn bring about this change. We will not have a new continent without new and reformed structures, but, above all, there will be no new continent without new men, who know how to be truly free and responsible according to the light of the Gospel.

4. Only by the light of Christ is the mystery of man made clear. In the economy of salvation the divine work is an action of integral human development and liberation, which has love for its sole motive. Man is "created in Christ Jesus" (Eph. 2:10), fashioned in Him as a "new creature" (2 Cor. 5:17). By faith and baptism he is transformed, filled with the gift of the Spirit, with a new dynamism, not of selfishness, but of love which compels him to seek out a new, more profound relationship with God, his fellow man, and created things.

Love, "the fundamental law of human perfection, and therefore of the transformation of the world" (GS 38), is not only the greatest commandment of the Lord; it is also the dynamism which ought to motivate Christians to realize justice in the world, having truth as a foundation and liberty as their sign.

5. This is how the Church desires to serve the world, radiating over it a light and life which heals and elevates the dignity of the human person (GS 41), which consolidates the unity of society (GS 42) and gives a more profound reason and meaning to all human activity.

Doubtless, for the Church, the fullness and perfection of the human vocation will be accomplished with the definitive inclusion of each man in the Passover or Triumph of Christ, but the hope of such a definitive realization, rather than lull, ought to "vivify the concern to perfect this earth. For here grows the body of the new human family, a body which even now is able to give some kind of foreshadowing of the new age" (GS 39). We do not confuse temporal progress and the Kingdom of Christ; nevertheless, the former, "to the extent that it can contribute to the better ordering of human society, is of vital concern to the Kingdom of God" (GS 39).

The Christian quest for justice is a demand arising from biblical teaching. All men are merely humble stewards of material goods. In the search for salvation we must avoid the dualism which separates temporal tasks from the work of sanctification. Although we are encompassed with imperfections, we are men of hope. We have faith that our love for Christ and our brethren will not only be the great force liberating us from injustice and oppression, but also the inspiration for social justice, understood as a whole of life and as an impulse toward the integral growth of our countries.

III. PROJECTIONS FOR SOCIAL PASTORAL PLANNING

6. Our pastoral mission is essentially a service of encouraging and educating the conscience of believers, to help them to perceive the responsibilities of their faith in their personal life and in their social life. This Second Episcopal Conference wishes to point out the most important demands, taking into account the value judgment which the latest Documents of the Magisterium of the Church have already made concerning the economic and social situation of the world of today and which applies fully to the Latin American continent.

Direction of Social Change

7. The Latin American Church encourages the formation of national communities that reflect a global organization, where all of the peoples but more especially the lower classes have, by means of territorial and functional structures, an active and receptive, creative and decisive participation in the construction of a new society. Those intermediary structures—between the person and the state—should be freely organized, without any unwarranted interference from authority or from dominant groups, in view of their development and concrete participation in the accomplishment of the total common good. They constitute the vital network of society. They are also the true expression of the citizens' liberty and unity.

8. *The Family.* Without ignoring the unique character of the family, as the natural unit of society, we are considering it here as an intermediary structure, inasmuch as the families as a group ought to take up their function in the process of social change. Latin American families ought to organize their economic and cultural potential so that their legitimate needs and hopes be taken into account, on the levels where fundamental decisions are made, which can help or hinder them. In this way they will assume a role of effective representation and participation in the life of the total community.

Besides the dynamism which is generated in each country by the union of families, it is necessary that governments draw up legislation and a healthy and up-to-date policy governing the family.

9. *Professional Organization.* The Second Latin American Episcopal Conference addresses itself to all those who, with daily effort, create the goods and services which favor the existence and development of human life. We refer especially to the millions of Latin American men and women who make up the peasant and working class. They, for the most part, suffer, long for and struggle for a change that will humanize and dignify their work. Without ignoring the totality of the significance of human work, here we refer to it as an intermediary structure, inasmuch as it constitutes the function which gives rise to professional organization in the field of production.

10. *Business Enterprises and the Economy.* In today's world, production finds its concrete expression in business enterprises, the industrial as well as the rural; they constitute the dynamic and fundamental base of the integral economic process. The system of Latin American business enterprises, and through it the current economy, responds to an erroneous conception concerning the right of ownership of the means of production and the very goals of the economy. A business, in an authentically human economy, does not identify itself with the owners of capital, because it is fundamentally a community of persons and a unit of work, which is in need of capital to produce goods. A person or a group of persons cannot be the property of an individual, of a society, or of the state.

The system of liberal capitalism and the temptation of the Marxist system would appear to exhaust the possibilities of transforming the economic structures of our continent. Both systems militate against the dignity of the human person. One takes for granted the primacy of capital, its power, and its discriminatory utilization in the function of profit-making. The other, although it ideologically supports a kind of humanism, is more concerned with collective man, and in practice becomes a totalitarian concentration of state power. We must denounce the fact that Latin America sees itself caught between these two options and remains dependent on one or other of the centers of power which control its economy.

Therefore, on behalf of Latin America, we make an urgent appeal to the businessmen, to their organizations and to the political authorities, so that they might radically modify the evaluation, the attitudes, and the means regarding the goal, organization, and functioning of business. All those financiers deserve encouragement who, individually or through their organizations, make an effort to conduct their business according to the guidelines supplied by the social teaching of the Church. That the social and economic change in Latin America be channeled towards a truly human economy will depend fundamentally on this.

11. On the other hand this change will be essential in order to liberate the authentic process of Latin American development and integration. Many of our workers, although they gradually become conscious of the necessity for this change, simultaneously experience a situation of dependence on inhuman economic systems and institutions: a situation which, for many of them, borders on slavery, not only physical but also professional, cultural, civic, and spiritual.

With the clarity which arises from the knowledge of man and of his hopes, we must reiterate that neither the combined value of capital nor the establishment of the most modern techniques of production nor economic plans will serve man efficiently if the workers, the "necessary unity of direction" having been safeguarded, are not incorporated with all of the thrust of their humanity, by means of "the active participation of all in the running of the enterprise," according to ways which will have to be determined with care and on a macro-economic level, decisive nationally and internationally (GS 68).

12. *Organization of the Workers.* Therefore, in the intermediary professional structure the peasants' and workers' unions, to which the workers have a right, should acquire sufficient strength and power. Their associations will have a unified and responsible strength, to exercise the right of representation and participation on the levels of production and of national, continental, and international trade. They ought to exercise their right of being represented, also, on the social, economic, and political levels, where decisions are made which touch upon the common good. Therefore, the unions ought to use every means at their disposal to train those who are to carry out these responsibilities in moral, economic, and especially in technical matters.

13. *Unity of Action.* Socialization understood as a socio-cultural process of personalization and communal growth leads us to think that all of the sectors of society, but in this case principally the social-economic sphere, should, because of justice and brotherhood, transcend antagonisms in order to become agents of national and continental development. Without this unity, Latin America will not be able to succeed in liberating itself from the neo-colonialism to which it is bound, nor will Latin America be able to realize itself in freedom, with its own cultural, socio-political, and economic characteristics.

14. *Rural Transformation.* The Second Episcopal Conference wishes to voice its pastoral concern for the extensive peasant class, which, although included in the above remarks, deserves urgent attention because of its special characteristics. If it is true that one ought to consider the diversity of circumstances and resources in the different countries, there is no doubt that there is a common denominator in all of them: the need for the human promotion of the peasants and Indians. This uplifting will not be viable without an authentic and urgent reform of agrarian structures and policies. This structural change and its political implications go beyond a simple distribution of land. It is indispensable to make an adjudication of such lands, under detailed conditions which legitimize their occupation and insure their productivity for the benefit of the families and the national economy. This will entail, aside from juridical and technical aspects not within our compe-tence, the organization of the peasants into effective intermediate structures, principally in the form of cooperatives; and motivation towards the creation of urban centers in rural areas, which would afford the peasant population the benefits of culture, health, recreation, spiritual growth, participation in local decisions, and in those which have to do with the economy and national politics. This uplifting of the rural areas will contribute to the necessary process of industrialization and to participation in the advantages of urban civilization.

15. *Industrialization.* There is no doubt that the process of industrialization is irreversible and is a necessary preparation for an independent economy and integration into the modern world-wide economy. Industrialization will be a decisive factor in raising the standard of living of our countries and affording them better conditions for an integral development. Therefore it is indispensable to revise plans and reorganize national macro-economies, preserving the legitimate autonomy of our nation, and allowing for just grievances of the poorer nations and for the desired economic integration of the continent, respecting always the inalienable rights of the person and of intermediary structures, as protagonists of this process.

Political Reform

16. Faced with the need for a total change of Latin American structures, we believe that change has political reform as its prerequisite.

The exercise of political authority and its decisions have as their only end the common good. In Latin America such authority and decision-making frequently seem to support systems which militate against the common good or which favor privileged groups. By means of legal norms, authority ought effectively and permanently to assure the rights and inalienable liberties of the citizens and the free functioning of intermediary structures.

Public authority has the duty of facilitating and supporting the creation of means of participation and legitimate representation of the people, or if necessary the creation of new ways to achieve it. We want to insist on the necessity of vitalizing and strengthening the municipal and communal organization, as a beginning of organizational efforts at the departmental, provincial, regional, and national levels.

The lack of political consciousness in our countries makes the educational activity of the Church absolutely essential, for the purpose of bringing Christians to consider their participation in the political life of the nation as a matter of conscience and as the practice of charity in its most noble and meaningful sense for the life of the community.

Information and "Concientización"

17. We wish to affirm that it is indispensable to form a social conscience and a realistic perception of the problems of the community and of social structures. We must awaken the social conscience and communal customs in all strata of society and professional groups regarding such values as dialogue and community living within the same group and relations with wider social groups (workers, peasants, professionals, clergy, religious, administrators, etc.).

This task of *"concientización"* and social education ought to be integrated into joint Pastoral Action at various levels.

18. The sense of service and realism demands of today's hierarchy a greater social sensitivity and objectivity. In that regard there is a need for direct contact with the different social-professional groups in meetings which provide all with a more complete vision of social dynamics. Such encounters are to be regarded as instruments which can facilitate a collegial action on the part of the bishops, guaranteeing harmony of thought and activities in the midst of a changing society.

The National Episcopal Conference will implement the organization of courses, meetings, etc., as a means of integrating those responsible for social activities related to pastoral plans. Besides priests and interested religious and laymen, invitations could be extended to heads of national and international development programs within the country. In like manner the institutes organized to prepare foreign apostolic personnel will coordinate their activities of a pastoral-social nature with the corresponding national groups; moreover, opportunities will be sought for promoting study weeks devoted to social issues in order to articulate social doctrine applying to our problems. This will allow us to affect public opinion.

19. "Key men" deserve special attention; we refer to those persons at a decision-making level whose actions effect changes in the basic structures of national and international life. The Episcopal Conference, therefore, through its Commission on Social Action or Pastoral Service, will support, together with other interested groups, the organization of courses of study for technicians, politicians, labor leaders, peasants, managers, and educated men of all levels of society.

20. It is necessary that small basic communities be developed in order to establish a balance with minority groups, which are the groups in power. This is only possible through vitalization of these very communities by means of the natural innate elements in their environment.

The Church—the People of God—will lend its support to the down-trodden of every social class so that they might come to know their rights and how to make use of them. To this end the Church will utilize its moral strength and will seek to collaborate with competent professionals and institutions.

21. The Commission on Justice and Peace should be supported in all our countries at least at the national level. It should be composed of persons of a high moral caliber, professionally qualified and representative of different social classes; it should be capable of establishing an effective dialogue with persons and institutions more directly responsible for the decisions which favor the common good and detect everything that can wound justice and endanger the internal and external peace of the national and international communities; it should help to find concrete means to obtain adequate solutions for each situation.

22. For the implementation of their pastoral mission, the Episcopal Conferences will create Commissions on Social Action or Pastoral Service to develop doctrine and to take the initiative, presenting the Church as a catalyst in the temporal realm in an authentic attitude of service. The same applies to the diocesan level.

Furthermore, the Episcopal Conferences and Catholic organizations will encourage collaboration on the national and continental scene with non-Catholic Christian churches and institutions, dedicated to the task of restoring justice in human relations.

"Cáritas," which is a church organization (PP 46) integrated in the joint Pastoral Plan, will not be solely a welfare institution, but rather will become operational in the developmental process of Latin America, as an institution authentically dedicated to its growth.

23. The Church recognizes that these institutions of temporal activity correspond to the specific sphere of civic society, even though they are established and stimulated by Christians. In actual concrete situations this Second General Conference of Latin American Bishops feels it its duty to offer special encouragement to those organizations which have as their purpose human development and the carrying out of justice. The moral force of the Church will be consecrated, above all, to stimulate them, not acting except in a supplementary capacity and in situations that admit no delay.

Finally, this Second Conference is fully aware that the process of socialization, hastened by the techniques and media of mass communication, makes these means a necessary and proper instrument for social education and for *"concientización"* ordered to changing the structures and the observance of justice. For the same reason this Conference urges all, but especially laymen, to make full use of mass media in their work of human promotion.

APPENDIX B

Peace

Latin American Bishops
Medellín, 1968

Second General Conference Statement, Chapter Two

I. THE LATIN AMERICAN SITUATION AND PEACE

1. "If development is the new name for peace" (PP 87), Latin American underdevelopment, with its own characteristics in the different countries, is an unjust situation which promotes tensions that conspire against peace.

We can divide these tensions into three major groups, selecting, in each of these, those variables which constitute a positive menace to the peace of our countries by manifesting an unjust situation.

When speaking of injustice, we refer to those realities that constitute a sinful situation; this does not mean, however, that we are overlooking the fact that at times the misery in our countries can have natural causes which are difficult to overcome.

In making this analysis, we do not ignore or fail to give credit to the positive efforts made at every level to build a more just society. We do not include this here because our purpose is to call attention to those aspects which constitute a menace or negation of peace.

Tensions Between Classes and Internal Colonialism

2. *Different forms of marginality.* Socio-economic, cultural, political, racial, religious, in urban as well as rural sectors;

3. *Extreme inequality among social classes.* Especially, though not exclusively, in those countries which are characterized by a marked bi-classism, where a few have much (culture, wealth, power, prestige) while the majority has very little. The Holy Father describes this situation when directing himself to the Colombian rural workers; ". . . social and economic development has not been equitable in the great continent of Latin America; and while it has favored those who helped establish it in the beginning, it has neglected the masses of native population, which are almost always left at a subsistence level and at times are mistreated and exploited harshly" (Paul VI, Address to the Peasants, Mosquera, Colombia, August 23, 1968).

149

4. *Growing frustrations.* The universal phenomenon of rising expectations assumes a particularly aggressive dimension in Latin America. The reason is obvious: excessive inequalities systematically prevent the satisfaction of the legitimate aspirations of the ignored sectors, and breed increasing frustrations.

The same low morale is obtained in those middle classes which, when confronting grave crises, enter into a process of disintegration and proletarization.

5. *Forms of oppression of dominant groups and sectors.* Without excluding the eventuality of willful oppression, these forms manifest themselves most frequently in a lamentable insensitivity of the privileged sectors to the misery of the marginated sectors. Thus the words of the Pope to the leaders: "That your ears and heart be sensitive to the voices of those who ask for bread, concern, justice . . ." (Paul VI, Homily of the Mass on Development Day, Bogotá, August 23, 1968).

It is not unusual to find that these groups, with the exception of some enlightened minorities, characterize as subversive activities all attempts to change the social system which favors the permanence of their privileges.

6. *Power unjustly exercised by certain dominant sectors.* As a natural consequence of the above-mentioned attitudes, some members of the dominant sectors occasionally resort to the use of force to repress drastically any attempt at opposition. It is easy for them to find apparent ideological justifications (anti-communism) or practical ones (keeping "order") to give their action an honest appearance.

7. *Growing awareness of the oppressed sectors.* All the above results are even more intolerable as the oppressed sectors become increasingly aware of their situation. The Holy Father referred to them when he said to the rural workers: "But today the problem has worsened because you have become more aware of your needs and suffering, and you cannot tolerate the persistence of these conditions without applying a careful remedy" (Paul VI, Address to the Peasants, Mosquera, Colombia, August 23, 1968).

The static picture described in the above paragraphs is worsened when it is projected into the future: basic education will increase awareness, and the demographic explosion will multiply problems and tensions. One must not forget the existence of movements of all types interested in taking advantage of and irritating these tensions. Therefore, if today peace seems seriously endangered, the automatic aggravation of the problems will produce explosive consequences.

International Tensions and External Neocolonialism

8. We refer here, particularly, to the implications for our countries of dependence on a center of economic power, around which they gravitate. For this reason, our nations frequently do not own their goods, or have a say in economic decisions affecting them. It is obvious that this will not fail to have political consequences given the interdependence of these two fields.

We are interested in emphasizing two aspects of this phenomenon.

9. *Economic aspect.* We only analyze those factors having greater influence on the global and relative impoverishment of our countries, and which constitute a source of internal and external tensions.

a. *Growing distortion of international commerce.* Because of the relative depreciation of the terms of exchange, the value of raw materials is increasingly less in relation to the cost of manufactured products. This means that the countries which produce raw materials—especially if they are dependent upon one major export—always remain poor, while the industrialized countries enrich themselves. This injustice, clearly denounced by *Populorum Progressio* (56-61), nullifies the eventual positive effect of external aid and constitutes a permanent menace against peace, because our countries sense that "one hand takes away what the other hand gives" (PP 56).

b. *Rapid flight of economic and human capital.* The search for security and individual gain leads many members of the more comfortable sectors of our countries to invest their money in foreign countries. The injustice of such procedures has already been denounced categorically by the encyclical *Populorum Progressio* (24). To this can be added the loss of technicians and competent personnel, which is at least as serious and perhaps more so than the loss of capital, because of the high cost of training these people and because of their ability to teach others.

c. *Tax evasion and loss of gains and dividends.* Some foreign companies working in our country (also some national firms) often evade the established tax system by subterfuge. We are also aware that at times they send their profits and dividends abroad, without contributing adequate reinvestments to the progressive development of our countries.

d. *Progressive debt.* It is not surprising to find that in the system of international credits, the true needs and capabilities of our countries are not taken into account. We thus run the risk of encumbering ourselves with debts whose payment absorbs the greater part of our profits (PP 54).

e. *International monopolies and international imperialism of money.* We wish to emphasize that the principal guilt for economic dependence of our countries rests with powers, inspired by uncontrolled desire for gain, which leads to economic dictatorship and the "international imperialism of money" (PP 26) condemned by Pope Pius XI in *Quadragesimo Anno* and by Pope Paul VI in *Populorum Progressio.*

10. *Political aspect.* We here denounce the imperialism of any ideological bias exercised in Latin America either indirectly or through direct intervention.

Tensions Among the Countries of Latin America

11. We here denounce the particular phenomenon of historico-political origin that continues to disturb cordial relations among some countries and impedes truly constructive collaboration. Nevertheless, the integration process, well understood, presents itself as a commanding necessity for Latin America. Without pretending to set norms of a truly complex, technical nature, governing integration, we deem it opportune to point out its multi-dimensional character. Integration, in effect, is not solely an economic process; it has a broader dimension reflected in the way in which it embraces man in his total situation: social, political, cultural, religious, racial.

Among the factors that increase the tensions among our countries we under-line:

12. *An exacerbated nationalism in some countries.* The Holy Father (PP 62) has already denounced the unwholesomeness of this attitude, especially on a matter where the weakness of the national economies requires a union of efforts.

13. *Armaments.* In certain countries an arms race is under way that surpasses the limits of reason. It frequently stems from a fictitious need to respond to diverse interests rather than to a true need of the national community. In that respect, a phrase of *Populorum Progressio* is particularly pertinent: "When so many com-munities are hungry, when so many homes suffer misery, when so many men live submerged in ignorance . . . any arms race becomes an intolerable scandal" (PP 53).

II. DOCTRINAL REFLECTION

Christian View of Peace

14. The above mentioned Christian viewpoint on peace adds up to a negation of peace such as Christian tradition understands it.

Three factors characterize the Christian concept of peace:

a. Peace is, above all, a work of justice (GS 78). It presupposes and requires the establishment of a just order (PT 167; PP 76) in which men can fulfill themselves as men, where their dignity is respected, their legitimate aspirations satisfied, their access to truth recognized, their personal freedom guaranteed; an order where man is not an object, but an agent of his own history. Therefore, there will be attempts against peace where unjust inequalities among men and nations prevail (Paul VI, Message of January 1, 1968).

Peace in Latin America, therefore, is not the simple absence of violence and bloodshed. Oppression by the power groups may give the impression of maintain-ing peace and order, but in truth it is nothing but the "continuous and inevitable seed of rebellion and war" (Paul VI, Message of January 1, 1968).

"Peace can only be obtained by creating a new order which carries with it a more perfect justice among men" (PP 76). It is in this sense that the integral development of man, the path to more human conditions, becomes the symbol of peace.

b. Secondly, peace is a permanent task (GS 78). A community becomes a reality in time and is subject to a movement that implies constant change in structures, transformation of attitudes, and conversion of hearts.

The "tranquility of order," according to the Augustinian definition of peace, is neither passivity nor conformity. It is not something that is acquired once and for all. It is the result of continuous effort and adaptation to new circumstances, to new demands and challenges of a changing history. A static and apparent peace may be obtained with the use of force; an authentic peace implies struggle, creative abilities, and permanent conquest (Paul VI, Christmas Message, 1967).

Peace is not found, it is built. The Christian man is the artisan of peace

(Matt. 5:9). This task, given the above circumstances, has a special character in our continent; thus the People of God in Latin America, following the example of Christ, must resist personal and collective injustice with unselfish courage and fearlessness.

c. Finally, peace is the fruit of love (GS 78). It is the expression of true fraternity among men, a fraternity given by Christ, Prince of Peace, in reconciling all men with the Father. Human solidarity cannot truly take effect unless it is done in Christ, who gives Peace that the world cannot give (John 14:27). Love is the soul of justice. The Christian who works for social justice should always cultivate peace and love in his heart.

Peace with God is the basic foundation of internal and social peace. Therefore, where this social peace does not exist, there will we find social, political, economic, and cultural inequalities; there will we find the rejection of the peace of the Lord, and a rejection of the Lord himself (Matt. 25:31-46).

The Problem of Violence in Latin America

15. Violence constitutes one of the gravest problems in Latin America. A decision on which the future of the countries of the continent will depend should not be left to the impulses of emotion and passion. We would be failing in our pastoral duty if we were not to remind the conscience, caught in this dramatic dilemma, of the criteria derived from the Christian doctrine of evangelical love.

No one should be surprised if we forcefully reaffirm our faith in the productiveness of peace. This is our Christian ideal. "Violence is neither Christian nor evangelical" (Paul VI, Homily of the Mass on Development Day, Bogotá, August 23, 1968; Med-OA). The Christian man is peaceful and not ashamed of it. He is not simply a pacifist, for he can fight (Paul VI, Message of January 1, 1968), but he prefers peace to war. He knows that "violent changes in structures would be fallacious, ineffectual in themselves and not conforming to the dignity of man, which demands that the necessary changes take place from within, that is to say, through a fitting awakening of conscience, adequate preparation, and effective participation of all, which the ignorance and often inhuman conditions of life make it impossible to assure at this time" (Paul VI, Homily of the Mass on Development Day, Bogotá, 1968).

16. As the Christian believes in the productiveness of peace in order to achieve justice, he also believes that justice is a prerequisite for peace. He recognizes that in many instances Latin America finds itself faced with a situation of injustice that can be called institutionalized violence, when, because of a structural deficiency of industry and agriculture, of national and international economy, of cultural and political life, "whole towns lack necessities, live in such dependence as hinders all initiative and responsibility as well as every possibility for cultural promotion and participation in social and political life" (PP 30), thus violating fundamental rights. This situation demands all-embracing, courageous, urgent, and profoundly renovating transformations. We should not be surprised, therefore, that the "temptation to violence" is surfacing in Latin America. One should not abuse the patience of a people that for years has borne a situation that would not be acceptable to anyone with any degree of awareness of human rights.

Facing a situation which works so seriously against the dignity of man and against peace, we address ourselves, as pastors, to all the members of the Christian community, asking them to assume their responsibility in the promotion of peace in Latin America.

17. We would like to direct our call in the first place, to those who have a greater share of wealth, culture, and power. We know that there are leaders in Latin America who are sensitive to the needs of the people and try to remedy them. They recognize that the privileged many times join together and with all the means at their disposal pressure those who govern, thus obstructing necessary changes. In some instances, this pressure takes on drastic proportions which result in the destruction of life and property.

Therefore, we urge them not to take advantage of the pacifist position of the Church in order to oppose, either actively or passively, the profound transformations that are so necessary. If they jealously retain their privileges and defend them through violence, they are responsible to history for provoking "explosive revolutions of despair" (Paul VI, Homily of the Mass on Development Day, Bogotá, 1968). The peaceful future of the countries of Latin America depends to a large extent on their attitude.

18. Also responsible for injustice are those who remain passive for fear of the sacrifice and personal risk implied by any courageous and effective action. Justice, and therefore peace, conquer by means of a dynamic action of awakening *(concientización)* and organization of the popular sectors, which are capable of pressing public officials who are often impotent in their social projects without popular support.

19. We address ourselves finally, to those who, in the face of injustice and illegitimate resistance to change, put their hopes in violence. With Paul VI we realize that their attitude "frequently finds its ultimate motivation in noble impulses of justice and solidarity" (Paul VI, Homily of the Mass on Development Day, Bogotá, 1968). Let us not speak here of empty words which do not imply personal responsibility and which isolate from the fruitful non-violent actions that are immediately possible.

If it is true that revolutionary insurrection can be legitimate in the case of evident and prolonged "tyranny that seriously works against the fundamental rights of man, and which damages the common good of the country" (PP 31), whether it proceeds from one person or from clearly unjust structures, it is also certain that violence or "armed revolution" generally "generates new injustices, introduces new imbalances, and causes new disasters; one cannot combat a real evil at the price of a greater evil" (PP 31).

If we consider then, the totality of the circumstances of our countries, and if we take into account the Christian preference for peace, the enormous difficulty of a civil war, the logic of violence, the atrocities it engenders, the risk of provoking foreign intervention, illegitimate as it may be, the difficulty of building a regime of justice and freedom while participating in a process of violence, we earnestly desire that the dynamism of the awakened and organized community be put to the service of justice and peace.

Finally, we would like to make ours the words of our Holy Father to the newly ordained priests and deacons in Bogotá, when he referred to all the suffering and said to them: "We will be able to understand their afflictions and change them, not into hate and violence, but into the strong and peaceful energy of constructive works" (Paul VI, Address to New Priests and Deacons, Bogotá, August 22, 1968).

III. PASTORAL CONCLUSIONS

20. In the face of the tensions which conspire against peace, and even present the temptation of violence; in the face of the Christian concept of peace which has been described, we believe that the Latin American Episcopate cannot avoid assuming very concrete responsibilities; because to create a just social order, without which peace is illusory, is an eminently Christian task.

To us, the Pastors of the Church, belongs the duty to educate the Christian conscience, to inspire, stimulate, and help orient all of the initiatives that contribute to the formation of man. It is also up to us to denounce everything which, opposing justice, destroys peace.

In this spirit we feel it opportune to bring up the following pastoral points:

21. To awaken in individuals and communities, principally through mass media, a living awareness of justice, infusing in them a dynamic sense of responsibility and solidarity.

22. To defend the rights of the poor and oppressed according to the Gospel commandment, urging our governments and upper classes to eliminate anything which might destroy social peace: injustice, inertia, venality, insensibility.

23. To favor integration, energetically denouncing the abuses and unjust consequences of the excessive inequalities between poor and rich, weak and powerful.

24. To be certain that our preaching, liturgy, and catechesis take into account the social and community dimensions of Christianity, forming men committed to world peace.

25. To achieve in our schools, seminaries, and universities a healthy critical sense of the social situation and foster the vocation of service. We also consider very efficacious the diocesan and national campaigns that mobilize the faithful and social organizations, leading them to a similar reflection.

26. To invite various Christian and non-Christian communities to collaborate in this fundamental task of our times.

27. To encourage and favor the efforts of the people to create and develop their own grass-roots organizations for the redress and consolidation of their rights and the search for true justice.

28. To request the perfecting of the administration of justice, whose deficiencies often cause serious ills.

29. To urge a halt and revision in many of our countries of the arms race that at times constitutes a burden excessively disproportionate to the legitimate demands of the common good, to the detriment of desperate social necessities. The struggle against misery is the true war that our nations should face.

30. To invite the bishops, the leaders of different churches, and all men of good will of the developed nations to promote in their respective spheres of influence, especially among the political and financial leaders, a consciousness of greater solidarity facing our underdeveloped nations, obtaining, among other things, just prices for our raw materials.

31. On the occasion of the twentieth anniversary of the solemn declaration of Human Rights, to interest universities in Latin America to undertake investigations to verify the degree of its implementation in our countries.

32. To denounce the unjust action of world powers that works against self-determination of weaker nations who must suffer the bloody consequences of war and invasion, and to ask competent international organizations for effective and decisive procedures.

33. To encourage and praise the initiatives and works of all those who in the diverse areas of action contribute to the creation of a new order which will assure peace in our midst.

Evangelization, Liberation, and Human Promotion

Latin American Bishops
Puebla, 1979

Third General Conference Statement,
Part Two, Chapter Two, Section Four

In this section we shall discuss evangelization in terms of its connection with human promotion, liberation, and the social doctrine of the Church.

4.1. A Word of Encouragement

We fully recognize the efforts undertaken by many Latin American Christians to explore the particularly conflict-ridden situations of our peoples in terms of the faith and to shed the light of God's Word on them. We encourage all Christians to continue to provide this evangelizing service and to consider the criteria for reflection and investigation; and we urge them to put special care into preserving and promoting ecclesial communion on both the local and the universal levels.

We are also aware of the fact that since the Medellín Conference pastoral agents have made significant advances and encountered quite a few difficulties. Rather than discouraging us, this should inspire us to seek out new paths and better forms of accomplishment.

4.2. The Social Teaching of the Church

The contribution of the Church to liberation and human promotion has gradually been taking shape in a series of doctrinal guidelines and criteria for action that we now are accustomed to call "the social teaching of the Church." These teachings have their source in Sacred Scripture, in the teaching of the Fathers and major theologians of the Church, and in the magisterium (particularly that of the most recent popes). As is evident from their origin, they contain permanently valid elements that are grounded in an anthropology that derives from the message of Christ and in the perennial values of Christian ethics. But they also contain changing elements that correspond to the particular conditions of each country and each epoch.

Following Paul VI (OA 4), we can formulate the matter this way: attentive to the signs of the time, which are interpreted in the light of the Gospel and the Church's magisterium, the whole Christian community is called upon to assume responsibility for concrete options and their effective implementation in order to respond to the summons presented by changing circumstances. Thus these social teachings possess a dynamic character. In their elaboration and application lay people are not to be passive executors but rather active collaborators with their pastors, contributing their experience as Christians, and their professional, scientific competence (GS 42).

Clearly, then, it is the whole Christian community, in communion with its legitimate pastors and guided by them, that is the responsible subject of evangelization, liberation, and human promotion.

The primary object of this social teaching is the personal dignity of the human being, who is the image of God, and the protection of all inalienable human rights (PP 14-21). As the need has arisen, the Church has proceeded to spell out its teaching with regard to other areas of life: social life, economics, politics, and cultural life. But the aim of this doctrine of the Church, which offers its own specific vision of the human being and humanity (PP 13), is always the promotion and integral liberation of human beings in terms of both their earthly and their transcendent dimensions. It is a contribution to the construction of the ultimate and definitive Kingdom, although it does not equate earthly progress with Christ's Kingdom (GS 39).

If our social teachings are to be credible and to be accepted by all, they must effectively respond to the serious challenges and problems arising out of the reality of Latin America. Human beings who are diminished by all sorts of deficiencies and wants are calling for urgent efforts of promotion on our part, and this makes our works of social assistance necessary. Nor can we propose our teaching without being challenged by it in turn insofar as our personal and institutional behavior is concerned. It requires us to display consistency, creativity, boldness, and total commitment. Our social conduct is an integral part of our following of Christ. Our reflection on the Church's projection into the world as a sacrament of communion and salvation is a part of our theological reflection. For "evangelization would not be complete if it did not take into account the reciprocal appeal that arises in the course of time between the Gospel on the one hand and the concrete personal and social life of human beings on the other" (EN 29).

Human promotion entails activities that help to arouse human awareness in every dimension and to make human beings themselves the active protagonists of their own human and Christian development. It educates people in living together, it gives impetus to organization, it fosters Christian sharing of goods, and it is an effective aid to communion and participation.

If the Christian community is to bear consistent witness in its efforts for liberation and human betterment, each country and local church will organize its social pastoral effort around ongoing and adequate organisms. These organisms will sustain and stimulate commitment to the community, ensuring the needed coordination of activities through a continuing dialogue with all the members of the Church. Caritas and other organisms, which have been doing effective work for many years, can offer valuable help to this end.

If they are to be faithful and complete, theology, preaching, and catechesis must keep in mind the whole human being and all human beings. In timely and adequate terms they must offer people today "an especially vigorous message concerning liberation" (EN 29), framing it in terms of the "overall plan of salvation" (EN 38). So it seems that we must offer some clarifying remarks about the concept of liberation itself at this present moment in the life of our continent.

4.3. Discerning the Nature of Liberation in Christ

At the Medellín Conference we saw the elucidation of a dynamic process of integral liberation. Its positive echoes were taken up by *Evangelii Nuntiandi* and by John Paul II in his message to this conference. This proclamation imposes an urgent task on the Church, and it belongs to the very core of an evangelization that seeks the authentic realization of the human being.

But there are different conceptions and applications of liberation. Though they share common traits, they contain points of view that can hardly be brought together satisfactorily. The best thing to do, therefore, is to offer criteria that derive from the magisterium and that provide us with the necessary discernment regarding the original conception of Christian liberation.

There are two complementary and inseparable elements. The first is liberation from all the forms of bondage, from personal and social sin, and from everything that tears apart the human individual and society; all this finds its source to be in egotism, in the mystery of iniquity. The second element is liberation for progressive growth in being through communion with God and other human beings; this reaches its culmination in the perfect communion of heaven, where God is all in all and weeping forever ceases.

This liberation is gradually being realized in history, in our personal history and that of our peoples. It takes in all the different dimensions of life: the social, the political, the economic, the cultural, and all their interrelationships. Through all these dimensions must flow the transforming treasure of the Gospel. It has its own specific and distinctive contribution to make, which must be safeguarded. Otherwise we would be faced with the situation described by Paul VI in *Evangelii Nuntiandi:* "The Church would lose its innermost significance. Its message of liberation would have no originality of its own. It would be prone to takeover or manipulation by ideological systems and political parties" (EN 32).

It should be made clear that this liberation is erected on the three great pillars that John Paul II offered us as defining guidelines: i.e., the truth about Jesus Christ, the truth about the Church, and the truth about human beings.

Thus we mutilate liberation in an unpardonable way if we do not achieve liberation from sin and all its seductions and idolatry, and if we do not help to make concrete the liberation that Christ won on the cross. We do the very same thing if we forget the crux of liberative evangelization, which is to transform human beings into active subjects of their own individual and communitarian development. And we also do the very same thing if we overlook dependence and the forms of bondage that violate basic rights that come from God, the Creator and Father, rather than being bestowed by governments or institutions, however powerful they may be.

The sort of liberation we are talking about knows how to use evangelical means, which have their own distinctive efficacy. It does not resort to violence of any sort, or to the dialectics of class struggle. Instead it relies on the vigorous energy and activity of Christians, who are moved by the Spirit to respond to the cries of countless millions of their brothers and sisters.

We pastors in Latin America have the most serious reasons for pressing for liberative evangelization. It is not just that we feel obliged to remind people of individual and social sinfulness. The further reason lies in the fact that since the Medellín Conference the situation has grown worse and more acute for the vast majority of our population.

We are pleased to note many examples of efforts to live out liberative evangelization in all its fullness. One of the chief tasks involved in continuing to encourage Christian liberation is the creative search for approaches free of ambiguity and reductionism (EN 32) and fully faithful to the Word of God. Given to us in the Church, that Word stirs us to offer joyful proclamation to the poor as one of the messianic signs of Christ's Kingdom.

John Paul II has made this point well: "There are many signs that help us to distinguish when the liberation in question is Christian and when, on the other hand, it is based on ideologies that make it inconsistent with an evangelical view of humanity, of things, and of events (EN 35). These signs derive from the content that the evangelizers proclaim or from the concrete attitudes that they adopt. At the level of content one must consider how faithful they are to the Word of God, to the Church's living tradition, and to its magisterium. As for attitudes, one must consider what sense of communion they feel, with the bishops first of all, and then with the other sectors of God's People. Here one must also consider what contribution they make to the real building up of the community; how they channel their love into caring for the poor, the sick, the dispossessed, the neglected, and the oppressed; and how, discovering in these people the image of the poor and suffering Jesus, they strive to alleviate their needs and to serve Christ in them (LG 8). Let us make no mistake about it: as if by some evangelical instinct, the humble and simple faithful spontaneously sense when the Gospel is being served in the Church and when it is being eviscerated and asphyxiated by other interests" (OAP III, 6).

Those who hold to the vision of humanity offered by Christianity also take on the commitment not to measure the sacrifice it costs to ensure that all will enjoy the status of authentic children of God and brothers and sisters in Jesus Christ. Thus liberative evangelization finds its full realization in the communion of all in Christ, as the Father of all people wills.

4.4. Liberative Evangelization for a Human Societal Life Worthy of the Children of God

Other than God, nothing is divine or worthy of worship. Human beings fall into slavery when they divinize or absolutize wealth, power, the state, sex, pleasure, or anything created by God—including their own being or human reason. God himself is the source of radical liberation from all forms of idolatry, because the adoration of what is not adorable and the absolutization of the relative leads to violation of the innermost reality of human persons: i.e., their relationship with God and their personal fulfillment. Here is the liberative word par excellence: "You shall do homage to the Lord your God; him alone shall you adore" (Matt. 4:10; cf. Deut. 5:6 ff.). The collapse of idols restores to human beings their essential realm of freedom. God, who is supremely free, wants to enter into dialogue with free beings who are capable of making their own choices and exercising their responsibilities on both the individual and communitarian levels. So we have a human history that, even though it possesses its own consistency and autonomy, is called upon to be consecrated to God by humanity. Authentic liberation frees us from oppression so that we can say yes to a higher good.

Humanity and earthly goods. By virtue of their origin and nature, by the will of the Creator, worldly goods and riches are meant to serve the utility and progress of each and every human being and people. Thus each and every one enjoys a primary, fundamental, and absolutely inviolable right to share in the use of these goods, insofar as that is necessary for the worthy fulfillment of the human person. All other rights, including the right of property and free trade, are subordinate to that right. As John Paul II teaches: "There is a social mortage on all private property" (OAP III, 4). To be compatible with primordial human rights, the right of ownership must be primarily a right of use and administration; and though this does not rule out ownership and control, it does not make these absolute or unlimited. Ownership should be a source of freedom for all, but never a source of domination or special privilege. We have a grave and pressing duty to restore this right to its original and primary aim (PP 23).

Liberation from the idol of wealth. Earthly goods become an idol and a serious obstacle to the Kingdom of God (Matt. 19:23-26) when human beings devote all their attention to possessing them or even coveting them. Then earthly goods turn into an absolute, and "you cannot give yourself to God and money" (Luke 16:13).

Turned into an absolute, wealth is an obstacle to authentic freedom. The cruel contrast between luxurious wealth and extreme poverty, which is so visible throughout our continent and which is further aggravated by the corruption that often invades public and professional life, shows the great extent to which our nations are dominated by the idol of wealth.

These forms of idolatry are concretized in two opposed forms that have a common root. One is liberal capitalism. The other, a reaction against liberal capitalism, is Marxist collectivism. Both are forms of what can be called "institutionalized injustice."

Finally, as already noted, we must take cognizance of the devastating effects of an uncontrolled process of industrialization and a process of urbanization that is taking on alarming proportions. The depletion of our natural resources and the pollution of the environment will become a critical problem. Once again we affirm that the consumptionist tendencies of the more developed nations must undergo a thorough revision. They must take into account the elementary needs of the poor peoples who constitute the majority of the world's population.

The new humanism proclaimed by the Church, which rejects all forms of idolatry, "will enable our contemporaries to enjoy the higher values of love and friendship, of prayer and contemplation, and thus find themselves. This is what will guarantee humanity's authentic development—its transition from less than human conditions to truly human ones" (PP 20). In this way economic planning will be put in the service of human beings rather than human beings being put in the service of economics (PP 34). The latter is what happens in the two forms of idolatry mentioned above (liberal capitalism and Marxist collectivism). The former is the only way to make sure that what human beings "have" does not suffocate what they "are" (GS 35).

Human beings and power. The various forms of power in society are a basic part of the order of creation. Hence in themselves they are essentially good, insofar as they render service to the human community.

Authority, which is necessary in every society, comes from God (Rom. 13:1; John 19:11). It is the faculty of giving commands in accordance with right reason. Hence its obligatory force derives from the moral order (PT 47), and it should develop out of that ground in order to oblige people in conscience: "Authority is before all else a moral force" (PT 48; GS 74).

Sin corrupts humanity's use of power, leading people to abuse the rights of others, sometimes in more or less absolute ways. The most notorious example of this is the exercise of political power. For this is an area that involves decisions governing the overall organization of the community's temporal welfare, and it readily lends itself to abuses. Indeed it may lead not only to abuses by those in power but also to the absolutizing of power itself (GS 73) with the backing of public force. Political power is divinized when in practice it is regarded as absolute. Hence the totalitarian use of power is a form of idolatry; and as such, the Church completely rejects it (GS 75). We grieve to note the presence of many authoritarian and even oppressive regimes on our continent. They constitute one of the most serious obstacles to the full development of the rights of persons, groups, and even nations.

Unfortunately, in many instances this reaches the point where the political and economic authorities of our nations are themselves made subject to even more powerful centers that are operative on an international scale. This goes far beyond the normal range of mutual relationships. And the situation is further aggravated by the fact that these centers of power are ubiquitous, covertly organized, and easily capable of evading the control of governments and even international organisms.

There is an urgent need to liberate our peoples from the idol of absolutized power so that they may live together in a society based on justice and freedom. As a youthful people with a wealth of culture and tradition, Latin Americans must carry out the mission assigned to them by history. But if they are to do this, they need a political order that will respect human dignity and ensure harmony and peace to the community, both in its internal relations and in its relations with other communities. Among all the aspirations of our peoples, we would like to stress the following:

—Equality for all citizens. All have the right and the duty to participate in the destiny of their society and to enjoy equality of opportunity, bearing their fair share of the burdens and obeying legitimately established laws.

—The exercise of their freedoms. These should be protected by basic institutions that will stand surety for the common good and respect the fundamental rights of persons and associations.

—Legitimate self-determination for our peoples. This will permit them to organize their lives in accordance with their own genius and history (GS 74) and to cooperate in a new international order.

—The urgent necessity of re-establishing justice. We are not talking only about theoretical justice recognized merely in the abstract. We are talking also about a justice that is effectively implemented in practice by institutions that are truly operative and adequate to the task.

Evangelization, Ideologies, and Politics

Latin American Bishops
Puebla, 1979

Third General Conference Statement,
Part Two, Chapter Two, Section Five

5.1. Introduction

Recent years have seen a growing deterioration in the sociopolitical life of our countries.

They are experiencing the heavy burden of economic and institutional crises, and clear symptoms of corruption and violence.

The violence is generated and fostered by two factors: (1) what can be called institutionalized injustice in various social, political, and economic systems; and (2) ideologies that use violence as a means to win power.

The latter in turn causes the proliferation of governments based on force, which often derive their inspiration from the ideology of National Security.

As a mother and teacher whose expertise is humanity, the Church must examine the conditions, systems, ideologies, and political life of our continent— shedding light on them from the standpoint of the Gospel and its own social teaching. And this must be done even though it knows that people will try to use its message as their own tool.

So the Church projects the light of its message on politics and ideologies, as one more form of service to its peoples and as a sure line of orientation for all those who must assume social responsibilities in one form or another.

5.2. Evangelization and Politics

The political dimension is a constitutive dimension of human beings and a relevant area of human societal life. It has an all-embracing aspect because its aim is the common welfare of society. But that does not mean that it exhausts the gamut of social relationships.

Far from despising political activity, the Christian faith values it and holds it in high esteem.

Speaking in general, and without distinguishing between the roles that may be proper to its various members, the Church feels it has a duty and a right to be present in this area of reality. For Christianity is supposed to evangelize the whole of human life, including the political dimension. So the Church criticizes those who would restrict the scope of faith to personal or family life; who would exclude the professional, economic, social, and political orders as if sin, love, prayer, and pardon had no relevance in them.

The fact is that the need for the Church's presence in the political arena flows from the very core of the Christian faith. That is to say, it flows from the lordship of Christ over the whole of life. Christ sets the seal on the definitive brotherhood of humanity, wherein every human being is of equal worth: "All are one in Christ Jesus" (Gal. 3:28).

From the integral message of Christ there flows an original anthropology and theology that takes in "the concrete personal and social life of the human being" (EN 29). It is a liberating message because it saves us from the bondage of sin, which is the root and source of all oppression, injustice, and discrimination.

These are some of the reasons why the Church is present in the political arena to enlighten consciences and to proclaim a message that is capable of transforming society.

The Church recognizes the proper autonomy of the temporal order (GS 36). This holds true for governments, parties, labor unions, and other groups in the social and political arena. The purpose that the Lord assigned to his Church is a religious one; so when it does intervene in the sociopolitical arena, it is not prompted by any aim of a political, economic, or social nature. "But out of this religious mission itself come a function, a light, and an energy which can serve to structure and consolidate the human community according to the divine law" (GS 42).

Insofar as the political arena is concerned, the Church is particularly interested in distinguishing between the specific functions of the laity, religious, and those who minister to the unity of the Church—i.e., the bishop and his priests.

5.3. Notions of Politics and Political Involvement

We must distinguish between two notions of politics and political involvement. First, in the broad sense politics seeks the common good on both the national and international plane. Its task is to spell out the fundamental values of every community—internal concord and external security—reconciling equality with freedom, public authority with the legitimate autonomy and participation of individual persons and groups, and national sovereignty with international coexistence and solidarity. It also defines the ethics and means of social relationships. In this broad sense politics is of interest to the Church, and hence to its pastors, who are ministers of unity. It is a way of paying worship to the one and only God by simultaneously desacralizing and consecrating the world to him (LG 34).

So the Church helps to foster the values that should inspire politics. In every nation it interprets the aspirations of the people, especially the yearnings of those that society tends to marginalize. And it does this with its testimony, its teaching, and its varied forms of pastoral activity.

Second, the concrete performance of this fundamental political task is normally carried out by groups of citizens. They resolve to pursue and exercise political power in order to solve economic, political, and social problems in accordance with their own criteria or ideology. Here, then, we can talk about "party politics." Now even though the ideologies elaborated by such groups may be inspired by Christian doctrine, they can come to differing conclusions. No matter how deeply inspired in church teaching, no political party can claim the right to represent all the faithful because its concrete program can never have absolute value for all (cf. Pius XI, *Catholic Action and Politics,* 1937).

Party politics is properly the realm of lay people (GS 43). Their lay status entitles them to establish and organize political parties, using an ideology and strategy that is suited to achieving their legitimate aims.

In the social teaching of the Church lay people find the proper criteria deriving from the Christian view of the human being. For its part the hierarchy will demonstrate its solidarity by contributing to their adequate formation and their spiritual life, and also by nurturing their creativity so that they can explore options that are increasingly in line with the common good and the needs of the weakest.

Pastors, on the other hand, must be concerned with unity. So they will divest themselves of every partisan political ideology that might condition their criteria and attitudes. They then will be able to evangelize the political sphere as Christ did, relying on the Gospel without any infusion of partisanship or ideologization. Christ's Gospel would not have had such an impact on history if he had not proclaimed it as a religious message: "The Gospels show clearly that for Jesus anything that would alter his mission as the Servant of Yahweh was a temptation (Matt. 4:8; Luke 4:5). He does not accept the position of those who mixed the things of God with merely political attitudes (Matt. 22:21; Mark 12:17; John 18:36)" (OAP I, 4).

Priests, also ministers of unity, and deacons must submit to the same sort of personal renunciation. If they are active in party politics, they will run the risk of absolutizing and radicalizing such activity; for their vocation is to be "men dedicated to the Absolute." As the Medellín Conference pointed out: "In the economic and social order . . . and especially in the political order, where a variety of concrete choices is offered, the priest, as priest, should not directly concern himself with decisions or leadership nor with the structuring of solutions" (Med-PR 19). And the 1971 Synod of Bishops stated: "Leadership or active militancy on behalf of any political party is to be excluded by every priest unless, in concrete and exceptional circumstances, this is truly required by the good of the community and receives the consent of the bishop after consultation with the priests' council and, if circumstances call for it, with the episcopal conference" ("The Ministerial Priesthood," Part Two, no. 2). Certainly the present thrust of the Church is not in that direction.

By virtue of the way in which they follow Christ, and in line with the distinctive function that is theirs within the Church's mission because of their specific charism, religious also cooperate in the evangelization of the political order. Living in a society that is far from fraternal, that is taken up with consumptionism, and that has as its ultimate goal the development of its material forces of production, religious will have to give testimony of real austerity in their lifestyle, of interhuman communion, and of an intense relationship with God. They, too, will have to resist the temptation to get involved in party politics, so that they do not create confusion between the values of the Gospel and some specific ideology.

Close reflection upon the recent words of the Holy Father addressed to bishops, priests, and religious will provide valuable guidance for their service in this area: "Souls that are living in habitual contact with God and that are operating in the warm light of his love know how to defend themselves easily against the temptations of partisanship and antithesis that threaten to create painful divisions. They know how to interpret their options for the poorest and for all the victims of human egotism in the proper light of the Gospel, without succumbing to forms of sociopolitical radicalism. In the long run such radicalism is untimely, counterproductive, and generative of new abuses. Such souls know how to draw near to the people and immerse themselves in their midst without calling into question their own religious identity or obscuring the 'specific originality' of their own vocation, which flows from following the poor, chaste, and obedient Christ. A measure of real adoration has more value and spiritual fruitfulness than the most intense activity, even apostolic activity. This is the most urgent kind of 'protest' that religious should exercise against a society where efficiency has been turned into an idol on whose altar even human dignity itself is sometimes sacrificed" (RMS).

Lay leaders of pastoral action should not use their authority in support of parties or ideologies.

5.4. Reflections on Political Violence

Faced with the deplorable reality of violence in Latin America, we wish to express our view clearly. Condemnation is always the proper judgment on physical and psychological torture, kidnapping, the persecution of political dissidents or suspect persons, and the exclusion of people from public life because of their ideas. If these crimes are committed by the authorities entrusted with the task of safeguarding the common good, then they defile those who practice them, notwithstanding any reasons offered.

The Church is just as decisive in rejecting terrorist and guerrilla violence, which becomes cruel and uncontrollable when it is unleashed. Criminal acts can in no way be justified as the way to liberation. Violence inexorably engenders new forms of oppression and bondage, which usually prove to be more serious than the ones people are allegedly being liberated from. But most importantly violence is an attack on life, which depends on the Creator alone. And we must also stress that when an ideology appeals to violence, it thereby admits its own weakness and inadequacy.

Our responsibility as Christians is to use all possible means to promote the implementation of nonviolent tactics in the effort to re-establish justice in economic and sociopolitical relations. This is in accordance with the teaching of Vatican II, which applies to both national and international life: "We cannot fail to praise those who renounce the use of violence in the vindication of their rights and who resort to methods of defense which are otherwise available to weaker parties too, provided that this can be done without injury to the rights and duties of others or of the community" (GS 78).

"We are obliged to state and reaffirm that violence is neither Christian nor evangelical, and that brusque, violent structural changes will be false, ineffective in themselves, and certainly inconsistent with the dignity of the people" (Paul VI, Address in Bogotá, August 23, 1968). The fact is that "the Church realizes that even the best structures and the most idealized systems quickly become inhuman if human inclinations are not improved, if there is no conversion of heart and mind on the part of those who are living in those structures or controlling them" (EN 36).

5.5. Evangelization and Ideologies

Here we shall consider the exercise of discernment with regard to the ideologies existing in Latin America and the systems inspired by them.

Of the many different definitions of ideology that might be offered, we apply the term here to any conception that offers a view of the various aspects of life from the standpoint of a specific group in society. The ideology manifests the aspirations of this group, summons its members to a certain kind of solidarity and combative struggle, and grounds the legitimacy of these aspirations on specific values. Every ideology is partial because no one group can claim to identify its aspirations with those of society as a whole. Thus an ideology will be legitimate if the interests it upholds are legitimate and if it respects the basic rights of other groups in the nation. Viewed in this positive sense, ideologies seem to be necessary for social activity, insofar as they are mediating factors leading to action.

But in themselves ideologies have a tendency to absolutize the interests they uphold, the vision they propose, and the strategy they promote. In such a case they really become "lay religions." People take refuge in ideology as an ultimate explanation of everything: "In this way they fashion a new idol, as it were, whose absolute and coercive character is maintained, sometimes unwittingly" (OA 28). In that sense it is not surprising that ideologies try to use persons and institutions as their tools in order to achieve their aims more effectively. Herein lies the ambiguous and negative side of ideologies.

But ideologies should not be analyzed solely in terms of their conceptual content. In addition, they are dynamic, living phenomena of a sweeping and contagious nature. They are currents of yearning tending toward absolutization, and they are powerful in winning people over and whipping up redemptive fervor.

This confers a special "mystique" on them, and it also enables them to make their way into different milieus in a way that is often irresistible. Their slogans, typical expressions, and criteria can easily make their way into the minds of people who are far from adhering voluntarily to their doctrinal principles. Thus many people live and struggle in practice within the atmosphere of specific ideologies, without ever having taken cognizance of that fact. This aspect calls for constant vigilance and re-examination. And it applies both to ideologies that legitimate the existing situation and to those that seek to change it.

To exercise the necessary discernment and critical judgment with regard to ideologies, Christians must rely on "a rich and complex heritage, which *Evangelii Nuntiandi* calls the social doctrine, or social teaching, of the Church" (OAP III, 7).

This social doctrine or teaching of the Church is an expression of its "distinctive contribution: a global perspective on the human being and on humanity" (PP 13). The Church accepts the challenge and contribution of ideologies in their positive aspects, and in turn challenges, criticizes, and relativizes them.

Neither the Gospel nor the Church's social teaching deriving from it are ideologies. On the contrary, they represent a powerful source for challenging the limitations and ambiguities of all ideologies. The ever fresh originality of the gospel message must be continually clarified and defended against all efforts to turn it into an ideology.

The unrestricted exaltation of the state and its many abuses must not, however, cause us to forget the necessity of the functions performed by the modern state. We are talking about a state that respects basic rights and freedoms; a state that is grounded on a broad base of popular participation involving many intermediary groups; a state that promotes autonomous development of an equitable and rapid sort, so that the life of the nation can withstand undue pressure and interference on both the domestic and international fronts; a state that is capable of adopting a position of active cooperation with the forces for integration into both the continental and the international community; and finally, a state that avoids the abuse of monolithic power concentrated in the hands of a few.

In Latin America we are obliged to analyze a variety of ideologies:

a. First, there is capitalist liberalism, the idolatrous worship of wealth in individualistic terms. We acknowledge that it has given much encouragement to the creative capabilities of human freedom, and that it has been a stimulus to progress. But on the other side of the coin it views "profit as the chief spur to economic progress, free competition as the supreme law of economics, and private ownership of the means of production as an absolute right, having no limits nor concomitant social obligations" (PP 26). The illegitimate privileges stemming from the absolute right of ownership give rise to scandalous contrasts, and to a situation of dependence and oppression on both the national and international levels. Now it is true that in some countries its original historical form of expression has been attenuated by necessary forms of social legislation and specific instances of government intervention. But in other countries capitalist liberalism persists in its original form, or has even retrogressed to more primitive forms with even less social sensitivity.

b. Second, there is Marxist collectivism. With its materialist presuppositions, it too leads to the idolatrous worship of wealth—but in collectivist terms. It arose as a positive criticism of commodity fetishism and of the disregard for the human value of labor. But it did not manage to get to the root of that form of idolatry, which lies in the rejection of the only God worthy of adoration: the God of love and justice.

The driving force behind its dialectics is class struggle. Its objective is a classless society, which is to be achieved through a dictatorship of the proletariat; but in the last analysis this really sets up a dictatorship of the party. All the concrete historical experiments of Marxism have been carried out within the framework of totalitarian regimes that are closed to any possibility of criticism and correction. Some believe it is possible to separate various aspects of Marxism—its doctrine and its method of analysis in particular. But we would remind people of the teaching of the papal magisterium on this point: "It would be foolish and danger- ous on that account to forget that they are closely linked to each other; to embrace certain elements of Marxist analysis without taking due account of their relation with its ideology; and to become involved in the class struggle and the Marxist interpretation of it without paying attention to the kind of violent and totalitarian society to which this activity leads" (OA 34).

We must also note the risk of ideologization run by theological reflection when it is based on a praxis that has recourse to Marxist analysis. The consequences are the total politicization of Christian existence, the disintegration of the language of faith into that of the social sciences, and the draining away of the transcendental dimension of Christian salvation.

Both of the aforementioned ideologies—capitalist liberalism and Marxism— find their inspiration in brands of humanism that are closed to any transcendent perspective. One does because of its practical atheism; the other does because of its systematic profession of a militant atheism.

c. In recent years the so-called Doctrine of National Security has taken a firm hold on our continent. In reality it is more an ideology than a doctrine. It is bound up with a specific politico-economic model with elitist and verticalist features, which suppresses the broad-based participation of the people in political deci- sions. In some countries of Latin America this doctrine justifies itself as the defender of the Christian civilization of the West. It elaborates a repressive system, which is in line with its concept of "permanent war." And in some cases it expresses a clear intention to exercise active geopolitical leadership.

We fully realize that fraternal coexistence requires a security system to incul- cate respect for a social order that will permit all to carry out their mission with regard to the common good. This means that security measures must be under the control of an independent authority that can pass judgment on violations of the law and guarantee corrective measures.

The Doctrine of National Security, understood as an absolute ideology, would not be compatible with the Christian vision of the human being as responsible for carrying out a temporal project, and to its vision of the state as the administrator of the common good. It puts the people under the tutelage of military and political elites, who exercise authority and power; and it leads to increased inequality in sharing the benefits of development.

We again insist on the view of the Medellín Conference: "The system of liberal capitalism and the temptation of the Marxist system would appear to exhaust the possibilities of transforming the economic structures of our continent. Both systems militate against the dignity of the human person. One takes for granted the primacy of capital, its power, and its discriminatory utilization in the function of profit-making. The other, although it ideologically supports a kind of humanism, is more concerned with collective humanity, and in practice becomes a totalitarian concentration of state power. We must denounce the fact that Latin America finds itself caught between these two options and remains dependent on one or the other of the centers of power that control its economy" (Med-JU 10).

In the face of this situation, the Church chooses "to maintain its freedom with regard to the opposing systems, in order to opt solely for the human being. Whatever the miseries or sufferings that afflict human beings, it is not through violence, power-plays, or political systems but through the truth about human beings that they will find their way to a better future" (OAP III, 3). Grounded on this humanism, Christians will find encouragement to get beyond the hard and fast either-or and to help build a new civilization that is just, fraternal, and open to the transcendent. It will also bear witness that eschatological hopes give vitality and meaning to human hopes.

For this bold and creative activity Christians will fortify their identity in the original values of Christian anthropology. The Church "does not need to have recourse to ideological systems in order to love, defend, and collaborate in the liberation of the human being. At the center of the message of which the Church is the trustee and herald, it finds inspiration for acting in favor of brotherhood, justice, and peace; and against all forms of domination, slavery, discrimination, violence, attacks on religious liberty, and aggression against human beings and whatever attacks life" (OAP III, 2).

Finding inspiration in these tenets of an authentic Christian anthropology, Christians must commit themselves to the elaboration of historical projects that meet the needs of a given moment and a given culture.

Christians must devote special attention and discernment to their involvement in historical movements that have arisen from various ideologies but are distinct from them. The teaching of *Pacem in Terris* (PT 55, 152), which is reiterated in *Octogesima Adveniens,* tells us that false philosophical theories cannot be equated with the historical movements that originated in them, insofar as these historical movements can be subject to further influences as they evolve. The involvement of Christians in these movements imposes certain obligations to persevere in fidelity, and these obligations will facilitate their evangelizing role. They include:

   a. Ecclesial discernment, in communion with their pastors, as described in *Octogesima Adveniens* (OA 4).

   b. The shoring up of their identity by nourishing it with the truths of faith, their elaboration in the social teaching or doctrine of the Church, and an enriching life of prayer and participation in the sacraments.

c. Critical awareness of the difficulties, limitations, possibilities, and values of these convergences.

5.6. The Danger of the Church and Its Ministers' Activity Being Used as a Tool

In propounding an absolutized view of the human being to which everything, including human thought, is subordinated, ideologies and parties try to use the Church or deprive it of its legitimate independence. This manipulation of the Church, always a risk in political life, may derive from Christians themselves, and even from priests and religious, when they proclaim a Gospel devoid of economic, social, cultural, and political implications. In practice this mutilation comes down to a kind of complicity with the established order, however unwitting.

Other groups are tempted in the opposite direction. They are tempted to consider a given political policy to be of primary urgency, a precondition for the Church's fulfillment of its mission. They are tempted to equate the Christian message with some ideology and subordinate the fomer to the latter, calling for a "rereading" of the Gospel on the basis of a political option (OAP 1,4). But the fact is that we must try to read the political scene from the standpoint of the Gospel, not vice-versa.

Traditional integrism looks for the Kingdom to come principally through a stepping back in history and reconstructing a Christian culture of a medieval cast. This would be a new Christendom, in which there was an intimate alliance between civil authority and ecclesiastical authority.

The radical thrust of groups at the other extreme falls into the same trap. It looks for the Kingdom to come from a strategic alliance between the Church and Marxism, and it rules out all other alternatives. For these people it is not simply a matter of being Marxists, but of being Marxists in the name of the faith.

5.7. Conclusion

The mission of the Church is immense and more necessary than ever before, when we consider the situation at hand: conflicts that threaten the human race and the Latin American continent; violations of justice and freedom; institutionalized injustice embodied in governments adhering to opposing ideologies; and terrorist violence. Fulfillment of its mission will require activity from the Church as a whole: pastors, consecrated ministers, religious, and lay people. All must carry out their own specific tasks. Joined with Christ in prayer and abnegation, they will commit themselves to work for a better society without employing hatred and violence; and they will see that decision through to the end, whatever the consequences. For the attainment of a society that is more just, more free, and more at peace is an ardent longing of the peoples of Latin America and an indispensable fruit of any liberative evangelization.

Church Collaboration With the Builders of a Pluralistic Society

Latin American Bishops Puebla, 1979

*Third General Conference Statement,
Part Four, Chapter Three*

Through the proclamation of the Good News and through a radical conversion to justice and love, the Church collaborates in the work of transforming from within those structures of a pluralistic society that respect and promote the dignity of the human person, and that provide persons with the possibility of achieving their supreme vocation: communion with God and with each other (EN 18-20).

3.1. The Situation

We will focus simply on a few aspects that present a more direct challenge to our pastoral activity. In a sense this will serve as a synthesis of questions treated elsewhere in this document.

Since the Medellín Conference in particular, two clear tendencies can be discerned:

a. On the one hand there is a thrust toward modernization, entailing strong economic growth, growing urbanization on our continent, and the increasingly technological character of economic, political, military, and other structures.

b. On the other hand the tendency is toward the pauperization and growing exclusion of the vast majority of Latin Americans from production. So the poor people of Latin America yearn for a society with greater equality, justice, and participation on every level.

These contradictory tendencies favor the appropriation by a privileged minority of a large part of the wealth as well as the benefits created by science and culture. On the other hand they are responsible for the poverty of a large majority of our people, who are aware of being left out and of having their growing aspirations for justice and participation blocked. Yet we also see that the middle classes are growing in many countries of Latin America.

So there arises a grave structural conflict: "The growing affluence of a few people parallels the growing poverty of the masses" (OAP III, 4).

3.2. Doctrinal Criteria

We live in a pluralistic society where we find differing religions, philosophical conceptions, ideologies, and value systems. Incarnated in different historical movements, they propose to construct the society of the future while rejecting the tutelage of any court of appeal that cannot be called into question.

We know that the Church, which has a valuable collaborative effort to make in the construction of society, does not claim any competence to propose alternative models (GS 42, 76). So we adopt the following doctrinal criteria:

a. We do not claim any privilege for the Church. We respect the rights of all people and the sincerity of all convictions, having complete respect for the autonomy of terrestrial realities.

b. However, we demand for the Church the right to bear witness to its message and to use its prophetic word of annunciation and denunciation in an evangelical sense, i.e., to correct false images of society that are incompatible with the Christian vision.

c. We defend the rights of intermediary organisms under the principle of subsidiarity, including the rights of such organisms created by the Church itself, in collaborating to deal with everything that relates to the common good.

3.3 Pastoral Criteria

We advocate the following:

a. Moving beyond the differentiation between pastoral care of elites and pastoral care of the common people. Our pastoral effort is one single effort. It penetrates evangelizing "cadres" or "elites." It affects all areas of social life. It gives dynamism to the life of society and at the same time it places itself in society's service.

b. The specific responsibility of lay people in building up temporal society, as *Evangelii Nuntiandi* proposes (EN 70).

c. A preferential concern to defend and promote the rights of the poor, the marginalized, and the oppressed.

d. A preferential concern for young people on the part of the Church, which sees in them a force for the transformation of society.

e. The irreplaceable responsibility of the woman, whose collaboration is indispensable for the humanization of the processes of transformation. This is to guarantee that love is a dimension of life and change. Her involvement is also needed because her perspective is indispensable for the complete representation of the needs and hopes of the people.

3.4 Options and Courses of Pastoral Action

We know that the common people, in their total dimension and their own particular way, construct the pluralistic society through their own organizations. Facing this challenge, we realize that the mission of the Church is not restricted to exhorting the various social groups and professional categories to fashion a new society for and with the common people. Nor is it solely to motivate each group to make its specific contribution in an honest, competent way. The Church must also urge them to serve as agents of a general consciousness-raising about the common responsibility, in the face of a challenge that requires the participation of all.

We realize that structural transformation is the outward expression of inner conversion. We know that this conversion begins with ourselves. Without the witness of a converted Church, our word as pastors would be futile (EN 41).

We assume the necessity of an organic pastoral effort in the Church as a unified source of dynamism, if it is to be effective in an ongoing way. This would include, among other things, guiding principles, objectives, options, strategies, and practical initiatives.

Courses of Pastoral Action:
—The defense and advancement of the inalienable dignity of the person.

—The universal destiny of the goods created by God and produced by human beings. We cannot forget that "there is a social mortgage on all private property" (OAP III, 4).

—Recourse to the sources of divine strength to be found in assiduous prayer, meditation on the Word of God which constantly calls things into question, and participation in the Eucharist by the constructors of society. With their enormous responsibilities, they are surrounded by temptations to lock themselves into the realm of earthly realities without opening up to the demands of the Gospel.

—Led by the bishop, the Christian community must build a bridge of contact and dialogue with the builders of temporal society, in order to enlighten them with the Christian vision, stimulate them with significant gestures, and accompany them with effective actions (OA 4).

—This contact and dialogue, marked by an attitude of sincere, receptive listening, should consider the problematic issues brought by the constructors of society from their own temporal sphere. In this way we will be able to find the criteria, norms, and approaches that will enable us to deepen and concretize the Church's social teaching. Here we are referring to the elaboration of a social ethics capable of formulating Christian answers to the major problems of contemporary culture (OA 4). We exhort all to combat economic corruption on every level, both in the area of public administration and in the area of private business; for such corruption causes grave damage to the vast majority of the people.

—This dialogue calls for initiatives that will permit encounter and close relationship with all those who are collaborating in the construction of society, so that they may discover their complementarity and convergence. To this end, priority must be placed on working with those who have decision-making power. This is not to rule out the recognition that social tensions can have constructive value. Within the demands of justice, such tensions help to guarantee people's freedom and rights, particularly those of the weakest.

Insofar as *options, objectives, and strategies* are concerned, we would propose the following:

—To train people in the various pastoral sectors who will be capable of exercising leadership in them that can serve as a leaven of evangelization.

—To elaborate, with people in each sector, norms of Christian conduct that will be the object of reflection and application and that will be subject to ongoing re-examination and revision.

—To promote encounters that will bring together people from various pastoral sectors to share experiences and coordinate their activities.

—To encourage the elaboration of viable alternatives in our evangelizing activity that will be geared toward the Christian renovation of social structures.

—To promote the training of priests and deacons in specialized areas, and also new ministries entrusted to the laity that suit the pastoral needs of each sector.

—To develop specialized movements that will bring together the elements available for the evangelization of particular milieus.

—To be wise enough to value the resources of the poor, the lowly, the common people, and artisans for communicating the divine message.

—To preserve the natural resources created by God for all human beings, in order to hand them down as an enriching heritage to future generations.

Insofar as *practical initiatives* are concerned, the Church directs its word amicably and spontaneously to those whom it knows are among the people who need its guidance or encouragement and who are waiting for it. That is to say, it addresses those who elaborate, propagate, and implement ideas, values, and decisions:

—We remind politicians and people in government of the words of Vatican II: "God alone is the source of your authority and the foundation of your laws" (Closing Message to Rulers). And God is so through the mediation of the people. We affirm the nobility and dignity of involvement in an activity aimed at consolidating internal concord and external security. We encourage the sensible, intelligent activity of politicians to give the State better government, to achieve the common good, and to effectively reconcile freedom, justice, and equality in a truly participatory society. "In their proper spheres, the political community and the Church are mutually independent and self-governing. Yet, by a different title, each serves the personal and social vocation of the same human beings. This service can be more effectively rendered for the good of all, if each works better for wholesome mutual cooperation, depending on the circumstances of time and place" (GS 76).

—We ask the intellectual and university world to act with spiritual freedom, to carry out its creative function in an authentic way, to prepare itself for political education—which is quite distinct from mere politicization—and to satisfy the inner logic of reflection and the rigorous demands of scientific scholarship. For from this realm we expect to get projects and solid theoretical guidelines for the construction of the new society (Vatican II, Closing Message to Men of Thought and Science).

—We ask scientists, technical people, and the creators of technological society to nurture their scientific spirit with love for the truth so that they may investigate the riddles of the universe and gain dominion over the earth. We ask them to avoid the negative effects of a hedonistic society and the technocratic temptation; to apply the power of technology to the creation of goods and the invention of means designed to rescue humanity from underdevelopment. In particular, we expect from them research and investigation designed to effect a synthesis between science and faith. We urge all thinkers who are aware of the value of wisdom—the first and last source of which is the *Logos*—and who are concerned about the creation of a new humanism, to take into account the magnificent statement of *Gaudium et Spes:* "The future of the world stands in peril unless wiser men are forthcoming" (GS 15). For this we need a major effort at interdisciplinary dialogue between theology, philosophy, and the sciences with a view to a new synthesis.

—We urge those in charge of the communications media to draw up and respect a code of ethics governing information and communication; to realize that the instrumental neutrality of the media means they can be used for good or ill; and to serve the cause of truth, objectivity, education, and adequate knowledge about reality.

—We urge creators in the arts to intuit the directions in which humankind is heading; to anticipate and interpret its crises; to open up the esthetic dimension of human life; and to contribute to the personalization of concrete human beings.

—We ask jurists with their special expertise to reclaim and defend the value of the law in the relationship between rulers and ruled, and for the maintenance of proper discipline in society. We urge judges not to compromise their independence; to hand down fair, intelligent judgments; and, through their verdicts, to help educate the rulers and the ruled in the carrying out of their obligations and the knowledge of their rights.

—To workers we say: In a world of growing urbanization and industrialization the role of workers becomes increasingly important as "the chief artisans of the prodigious changes which the world is undergoing today" (Vatican II, Closing Message to Workers). So workers should commit their real-life experience to the search for new ideas, thus renewing themselves and contributing even more decidedly to the construction of the Latin America of the future. They should not forget what Pope John Paul II told them in his talk. It is the right of workers "to freely create organizations to defend and promote their interests, and to contribute to the common good in a responsible way" (AWM 3).

—To peasants we say: You are a dynamic force in the building of a more participatory society. Taking your side, John Paul II addressed the following words to those sectors who hold power: "To you, responsible officials of the people, power-holding classes who sometimes keep your lands unproductive when they conceal the food that so many families are doing without, the human conscience, the conscience of the peoples, the cry of the destitute, and above all the voice of God and the Church join me in reiterating to you that it is not just, it is not human, it is not Christian to continue certain situations that are clearly unjust. You must implement real, effective measures on the local, national, and international levels, following the broad line marked out by the encyclical *Mater et Magistra.* . . . Most beloved brothers and sisters and children: work for your advancement as human beings" (AO).

—We urge economists to contribute their creative thinking so that they can provide speedy answers for the basic demands of the human being and society. We urge business-owners to keep in mind the social function of business enterprises, to view them not only as elements of production and profit but also as communities of persons and elements of a pluralistic society, which are viable only when no excessive concentration of economic power exists.

—To those in the military we would reiterate what the Medellín Conference told them: "They have a mission to guarantee rather than inhibit the political liberty of citizens" (Med-PE). They should be mindful of their mission, which is to guarantee the peace and security of all. They should never abuse the force they possess. They should be defenders of the force of right and law. They should also foster a societal life that is free, participatory, and pluralistic.

—We urge public functionaries to carry out their work as a service. For the dignity of public life and public service lies in the fact that it is naturally directed to society, especially those who have less and thus are more dependent on the proper functioning of the public sector.

—Finally, we urge all to contribute to the normal functioning of society. We urge professional people and merchants to undertake their mission in a spirit of service to the people, who look to them for the defense of their lives and their rights and for the promotion of their well-being.

3.5. Conclusion

At the present juncture in Latin American history there can be rapid, thoroughgoing changes that will benefit all. In particular, they can benefit the poor, who are most affected, and young people, who will soon be responsible for the destiny of our continent.

To this end we propose that all people of good will be mobilized; that they join together with new hope for this immense task. We wish to hear them with keen sensitivity and to join them in their constructive work.

We look forward to combining forces with all our brothers and sisters who profess one and the same faith in Christ, even though they do not belong to the Catholic Church. We hope to elaborate points of convergence in an ongoing, progressive way so that we can hasten the arrival of the Kingdom of God.

To the children of the Church working hard in advanced outposts we wish to convey our confidence in their activity. They are to be our messengers of new hopes. We know that they will look to the Gospel, prayer, and the Eucharist as the sources of constant re-examination and revision in their lives and of God's strength to aid their work of transformation.

Church Activity on Behalf of the Person in National and International Society

Latin American Bishops Puebla, 1979

Third General Conference Statement, Part Four, Chapter Four

4.1. Introduction

Human dignity is an evangelical value, as John Paul II has reminded us; and the 1974 Synod of Bishops taught us that the promotion of justice is an integral part of evangelization.* Human dignity and the promotion of justice must be made real in the national and international order.

In concerning ourselves with realities on the national and international scenes, we do so with an attitude of service as pastors rather than from an economic, political or merely sociological standpoint. What we want to see between human beings is greater communion and sharing of all the goods that God has given us.

So we want to look at the status of human dignity and of the promotion of justice in the real situation of our Latin America. We want to reflect on this matter in the light of our faith and in the light of principles grounded on human nature itself, in order to discover the criteria and services that will guide our pastoral activity today and in the near future.

---

*"Evangelization would not be complete if it did not take into account the mutual challenge that takes hold in the course of time between the Gospel and the concrete personal and social life of the human being. Precisely for this reason evangelization includes an explicit message, adapted to suit differing situations and fleshed out constantly, about the rights and duties of every human person; about family life, without which personal progress is hardly possible; about society's community life; about international life; about peace, justice, and development; and, in our day, a particularly forceful message about liberation" (EN 29).

"If the Church gets involved in defending or promoting human dignity, it does so in accordance with its mission. For even though that mission is religious in character, and not social or political, it cannot help but consider human persons in terms of their whole being. In the parable of the Good Samaritan, the Lord outlined the model way of attending to all human needs (Luke 10:30 ff.); and he said that in the last analysis he will identify himself with the disinherited—the imprisoned, the hungry, and the abandoned—to whom we have offered a helping hand (Matt. 25:31 ff.). In these and other passages of the Gospel (Mark 6:35–44), the Church has learned that an indispensable part of its evangelization mission is made up of works on behalf of justice and human promotion. It has learned that evangelization and human promotion are linked together by very strong ties of an anthropological, theological, and charitable nature" (OAP III, 2).

4.2. Situation

On the national level. Let us recall some of the points that have already been brought up in other sections of this document:

The people of Latin America continue to live in a social situation that contradicts the fact that they inhabit a continent which is Christian for the most part. The contradictions existing between unjust social structures and the demands of the Gospel are quite evident.

There are many causes for this situation of injustice; but at the root of them all we find sin, both on the personal level and in structures themselves.

We are deeply pained to see that the situation of violence—which can be called institutionalized violence (either as subversion or as repression)—has worsened. Human dignity is being abused, even in its most basic rights.

In particular we must note that since the decade of the fifties, and despite certain achievements, the ample hopes for development have come to nothing. The marginalization of the vast majority and the exploitation of the poor has increased.

Failure to find fulfillment as human persons with fundamental rights begins even before birth. People are encouraged to avoid conception of children, and even to interrupt pregnancy by means of abortion. Lack of fulfillment continues with infant malnutrition, premature abandonment, and lack of medical attention, education, and housing. This fosters an ongoing situation of disorder, which not surprisingly leads to a proliferation of criminality, prostitution, alcoholism, and drug addiction.

With access to social goods and social services blocked in this general context, as well as access to political decision-making, there is an intensification of attacks on freedom of opinion, religious freedom, and physical integrity. Assassinations, disappearances, arbitrary imprisonment, acts of terrorism, kidnappings, and acts of torture throughout the continent indicate a complete lack of respect for the dignity of the human person. And some try to justify themselves in this, even going so far as to appeal to the demands of national security.

No one can deny the concentration of business ownership in the hands of a few, both in urban and rural areas; so there is an imperious need for real agrarian and urban reforms. Nor can anyone deny the concentration of power in the hands of civilian and military technocracies, which frustrate rightful claims for participation and guarantees in a democratic state.

On the international level. Latin Americans see a society growing more and more unbalanced insofar as shared social life is concerned. There are "mechanisms that are imbued with materialism rather than authentic humanism, and that therefore lead on the international level to the ever increasing wealth of the rich at the expense of the ever increasing poverty of the poor" (OAP III, 4). These mechanisms manifest themselves in a society that is often programmed in terms of egotism; in manipulations of public opinion; in invisible expropriations; and in new forms of supranational domination, since the gap between the rich nations and the poor nations grows greater. And we must add that in many cases the power of multinational businesses overrides the exercise of sovereignty by nations and their complete control over their natural resources.

Due to these new ways of operating, and to the exploitation caused by the organizational systems governing economics and international politics, the underdevelopment of our hemisphere can grow worse and even become permanent. We see it as a threat to the ideal of Latin American integration. This lamentable situation is motivated in large measure by nationalistic economic ambitions, by the paralysis of major plans for cooperation, and by new international conflicts.

Sociopolitical imbalance on the national and international levels is creating may displaced people. Such, for example, are the emigrants, whose numbers can reach unexpected proportions in the near future. To them we must add people who have been displaced for political reasons: e.g., those in political asylum, refugees, exiles, and all the various people lacking proper documentary identification. Living in a situation of total neglect or abandonment are the aged, the underprivileged, vagabonds, and the vast masses of peasants and indigenous peoples, "almost always abandoned in an ignoble standard of living, and sometimes trapped and exploited severely" (Paul VI, Address to the Peasants, Bogotá, August 23, 1968).

Finally, an integral part of this complex social problem is the increase in arms expenditures and the artificial creation of superfluous needs imposed on poor nations from abroad.

4.3. Criteria

In national society. The fulfillment of persons comes about through the exercise of their fundamental rights, as they are effectively recognized, protected, and promoted. Hence the Church, the expert in humanity, must be the voice of those who have no voice (of the person, of the community vis-à-vis society, and of the weak nations vis-à-vis the strong nations). Its proper role is one of teaching, denouncing, and serving in the interests of communion and participation.

Faced with the situation of sin, the Church has a duty to engage in denunciation. Such denunciation must be objective, courageous, and evangelical. Rather than condemning, it attempts to save both the guilty party and the victim. Such denunciation, made after prior agreement has been reached between pastors, appeals to the internal solidarity of the Church and the exercise of collegiality.

Enunciating the basic rights of the human person today and in the future is an indispensable part of the Church's evangelizing mission, and it will ever remain so. The Church proclaims the necessity of the following rights, among others, and their implementation:

Individual rights: the right to life (to be born, to responsible procreation), to physical and psychic integrity, to legal protection, to religious freedom, to freedom of opinion, to participation in goods and services, to fashioning one's own destiny, to access to ownership "and other forms of private control over material goods" (GS 71).

Social rights: the right to education, to association, to work, to housing, to health, to recreation, to development, to good government, to freedom and social justice, and to sharing in the decisions that affect the people and nations.

Emerging rights: the right to one's own image, to a good reputation, to privacy, to information and objective expression, to conscientious objection "provided the just requirements of public order are observed" (DH 4), and to one's own vision of the world.

However, the Church also teaches that recognition of these rights presupposes and imposes on the person "just as many respective duties. And rights as well as duties find their source, their sustenance, and their inviolability in the natural law, which grants or enjoins them" (PT 28).

In international society. The imbalance in international society and the necessity of safeguarding the transcendent character of the human person in a new international order compels the Church to urge the proclamation of certain rights and active efforts to *turn them into a reality.* These would include:

—The right to a just form of international coexistence between nations, with full respect for their economic, political, social, and cultural self-determination.

—The right of each nation to defend and promote its own interests vis-à-vis multinational enterprises. On the international level there is now a need for a set of statutes that will regulate the activities of such enterprises.

—The right to a new form of international cooperation that will re-examine the original terms and conditions of such cooperation.

—The right to a new international order with the human values of solidarity and justice.

This new international order will avert a society built on neo-Malthusian criteria. It will be grounded on legitimate human social needs. It will provide for a healthy pluralism, and for the adequate representation of minorities and intermediary groups, so that it will not be a closed circle of nations. It will preserve the common patrimony of humanity, particularly the oceans.

Finally, economic surpluses, the savings from disarmament, and all other wealth on which there is a "social mortgage," even on the international level, will have to be utilized for social purposes. They should ensure the free and direct access of the weakest to their integral development.

Recognizing that the peoples of Latin America share many values, needs, difficulties, and hopes in common, there is a particular need to promote a legitimate form of continental integration. Such integration would move beyond various forms of egotism and narrow-minded nationalism, would respect the legitimate autonomy and territorial integrity of each people, and would encourage self-limitations on arms expenditures.

4.4. Services

Besides proclaiming the dignity of human persons, their rights, and their duties, and besides denouncing violations of the human being, the Church must also engage in active service as an integral part of its evangelizing, missionary task. In common with all people of faith and good will, the Church should create an ethical conscience with regard to the major international problems. To this end:

—The Church bears evangelical witness to God as present in history; and it awakens in human beings an attitude of openness to communion and participation.

—In its own sphere it establishes organisms of social action and human promotion.

—Insofar as it can, it steps in where public authorities and social organizations are absent or missing.

—It summons the human community to re-examine and give new direction to international institutions, and to create new forms of protection based on justice that will ensure the authentically human advancement of the growing number of the needy.

We recommend collaboration between episcopal conferences for the study of pastoral problems, particularly those relating to justice, which go beyond the national level.

Insofar as the nameless and faceless members of society are concerned, the Church has a particular duty to take them in and help them; and also to restore their dignity and their human visage, "because when a human being's dignity is violated, the whole Church suffers" (Paul VI, January 1977).

The Church must try to ensure that this floating segment of humanity is reintegrated into society without losing its own set of values. It must look after the full restoration of their rights. It must help to ensure that those who do not exist in legal terms get the necessary documentation, so that all may have access to the integral development that they deserve by virtue of their dignity as human beings and as children of God. In this way the Church will cooperate in the task of guaranteeing human beings a dignified existence, one that will equip them to find fulfillment both within the family and in society.

Action by the Church is also needed so that the displaced and marginalized people of our time do not become permanent second-class citizens. For they are subjects with rights and with legitimate social aspirations. They have a right to adequate pastoral attention, in accordance with papal documents and the guidelines proposed at Latin American meetings dealing with pastoral aspects of migration.

The Church makes an urgent appeal to the conscience of peoples and to humanitarian organizations, asking that:

—The right of asylum be strengthened and made general. This genuinely Latin American institution (Treaty of Rio de Janeiro, 1942) is the modern-day form of the protection once offered by the Church.

—Countries increase their quotas for immigrants and refugees, speeding up the implementation of agreements and mechanisms of integration relating to these matters.

—The occupational problem be attacked at its roots with specific policies for landholding, production, and commercialization. These policies should take care of the urgent needs of the population and give laborers stable places in their situations.

—Fraternal cooperation between nations in time of catastrophes be encouraged.

—Amnesty be facilitated as a sign of reconciliation in order to achieve peace, in line with Paul VI's invitation when he proclaimed the Holy Year of 1975.

—Centers for the defense of the human person be created. The aim of their work would be "to have the barriers of exploitation removed. These barriers are frequently the product of intolerable forms of egotism, against which [people's] best efforts at advancement are dashed" (AO).

To all those persons who are afflicted and who are suffering from the violation of their rights, we send our words of understanding and encouragement. We urge those responsible for the common good to make a determined effort to remedy the causes of these situations and to create the conditions needed for an authentically human form of societal coexistence.

Notes

Liberation, Theology, and Proclamation
GUSTAVO GUTIERREZ

1. Cf. texts of different sectors of the Latin American Church in *Signos de renovación* (Lima, 1969) and *Signos de liberación* (Lima, 1973). For an analysis of these texts see Ronaldo Muñoz, *Nueva conciencia de la Iglesia en América Latina* (Santiago de Chile, 1973).

2. Cf. Eric Hobsbawn's classic work, *The Age of Revolution: Europe 1789-1848* (London, 1962).

3. In its early stages the industrial revolution received some impetus from the inventive work of artisans. Shortly after that it made dynamic progress following scientific advances.

4. Cf. reflections on the Kantian Enlightenment in his *Philosophy of History* and of Hegel in his *Lessons on the Philosophy of History*. On this subject cf. the classic work of Ernst Cassirer, *The Philosophy of the Enlightenment* (New York and London, 1959), and the more recent work of W. Oelmüller, *Die unbefriedigte Aufklärung* (Frankfurt, 1969). For a theological view consult, J. B. Metz, J. Moltmann, W. Oelmüller, *Kirche im Prozess der Aufklärung* (Mainz, 1970).

5. For the political options now being followed in Latin America by this liberating praxis see my *Theology of Liberation* (New York, 1973; London, 1974), chapters 6 and 7.

6. The theme of evangelical poverty is dealt with more fully in my *Theology of Liberation,* chapter 13.

7. Cf. R. Schnackenburg, *L'existence chrétienne selon la Nouveau Testament,* vol. 1 (Paris, 1971), p. 35.

8. For a broad view of these questions and of current paths in contemporary theology consult the valuable reflections of C. Geffré in *Un nouvel âge de la théologie* (Paris, 1972). See also H. Bouillard, "Exegèse, hermeneutique et théologie, problèmes de methode" in *Exegèse et hermeneutique* (Paris, 1971); and the precise analysis of J. P. Jossua, "Ensemblement du discours chrétien" in *Christus* (June 1973), pp. 345-54.

9. See J. Guichard's attempt to highlight these questions in "Foi chrètienne et théorie de la connaissance" in *Lumière et Vie* (June-August 1973), pp. 61-84.

10. Note in this perspective the reflections of Duns Scotus on theology as a

practical science. Cf. also the work of Frans v.d. Qudenrijn, *Kritische Theologie als Kritik der Theologie* (Munich-Mainz, 1972).

11. Y. Congar, a theologian with a profound ecclesial and pastoral sense, has often emphasized this link between theology and proclamation. See, e.g., *Situations et tâches de la théologie* (Paris, 1967).

12. "Sonship is *the* distinctive feature of the Kingdom of God, the sole, true one": from J. Jeremias, *Théologie du Nouveau Testament,* vol. 1, *La prédiction de Jésus* (Paris, 1973), p. 227.

13. "The biblical hermeneutic will differ according as we consider the God of the Bible as totally distinct, with nothing in common with the universe in which man is so profoundly integrated, or simply as the Other 'whose ways are not our ways' (Is. 55. 8), nor his thoughts our thoughts, but yet 'We are indeed his offspring' (Acts 17. 28)." Cazelles, *Ecriture, Parole et Esprit* (Paris, 1970), p. 76.

14. Cf. Karl Rahner's perspicacious and courageous remarks on a Church of the future in *Strukturwandel der Kirche als Aufgabe und Chance* (Freiburg, 1972).

The American Press Views Puebla

JAMES V. SCHALL, S.J.

1. "Charisma was not the word to describe what had happened. Returning to his homeland for the first time since he was chosen Pope last October, Karol Wojtyla, John Paul II, stirred an outpouring of trust and affection that no political leader in today's world could hope to inspire, let alone command" (*Time*, June 18, 1979, p. 28). Cf. Tad Szulc, "Politics and the Polish Pope," *The New Republic*, October 28, 1978, pp. 19-22.

2. Cf. George F. Will, "The Cross and the Red Star," *Newsweek*, October 30, 1979, p. 112. From the *Wall Street Journal:*

Our foreign relations are increasingly complicated by a factor which our policy planners seem ill-equipped to handle, namely religion. From the ferment in Iran and the Arab world to the new Pope, faith and theology are beginning to have some very practical consequences.

The impact of John Paul II is just beginning to be felt but it could lead to a profound revival of the moral attraction of the West. . . .

Anyone who hopes to understand the world, and policymakers in particular, will have to become conversant not only with the relations among states but with the relation of man and the Almighty [editorial, "The Religious Element," *The Wall Street Journal,* December 8, 1978].

3. "Dramatically, it would have been hard for Carter, in any event, to cause a major splash with the trip, coming as it did on top of the triumphant visit to the land of the Aztecs of Pope John Paul II. Catholic Mexico, where the Church has been officially oppressed for fifty years, threw open its arms and its heart to the man from Krakow, from a land where the Church has been oppressed for nearly thirty years" ("Down Mexico Way," *National Review*, March 2, 1979, p. 280).

4. Tad Szulc, "Homecoming for the Pope," *The New York Times Magazine*, May 27, 1979, p. 22.

5. Cf. these articles from the *New York Times:* Kenneth Briggs, June 5, 1979; George Vecsey, "Activist Prelates Assess Pope's Trip," February 4, 1979; George Vecsey, "Support of Bishops for Activism Seen," February 12, 1979; Kenneth Briggs, "John Paul II Has No Easy Answers for Latin America," February 4, 1979; George Vecsey, February 1, 1979; Kenneth Briggs, "Papal Journey," February 2, 1979.

6. "Did the Pope Apply the Brakes at Puebla?," *The Christian Century*, February 23, 1979, p. 203.

7. Cf. Penny Lernoux, "The Church Keeps the Faith," *The Nation*, March 3, 1979; Penny Lernoux, *The National Catholic Reporter*, February 9, 1979, p. 5.

8. Harvey Cox, "A Puebla Diary," *Commonweal*, May 16, 1979, p. 145.

9. Arthur Jones, "John Paul Faces Marxism at Puebla," *The National Catholic Reporter*, January 26, 1979, p. 12.

10. Editorial, "Half a Blessing," *Commonweal*, February 16, 1979, p. 69.

11. Editorial, "The Pope and the Theologies of Liberation," *America*, February 10, 1979, pp. 84, 85.

12. Louis Fleming, "Pope John Paul in Mexico," *The Los Angeles Times,* February 4, 1979.

13. Szulc, "Homecoming for the Pope," p. 46.

14. Leopold Tyrmand, "Poland, Marxism, and John Paul II," *The Wall Street Journal,* December 6, 1978, p. 18. See John Paul II, "Address to U.S. Bishops," *Origins,* November 23, 1978.

15. Editorial, "The Polish Pope in Poland," *The New York Times,* June 5, 1979.

16. Editorial, "The Pope at Puebla," *The Wall Street Journal,* January 26, 1979. From *U.S. News and World Report:*

Throughout his trip, the Pope held to his basic line: that a laity united by traditional religious fervor, as in his native Poland, is the best defense against repression and other evils.

On a personal basis, churchmen view the jubilant greetings he got from crowds in officially anticlerical Mexico as a clear sign that he can take bold stands—and emerge with broad public support [*U.S. News and World Report,* February 12, 1979, p. 60].

17. Dale Vree, "Putting on the Tiara," *National Review,* March 30, 1979, p. 424.

18. Tyrmand, *loc. cit.* Cf. the author's "Catholicism and Intelligence," *The Clergy Review,* London, July 1977.

19. Cf. the author's "Christianity and the 'Cures' of Poverty," *Christianity and Politics* (Boston: St. Paul Editions, 1981), pp. 178-212.

20. Cf. the author's "Rethinking the Nature of Government," *Modern Age,* Spring 1979; "From Catholic 'Social Doctrine' to the 'Kingdom of God' on Earth," *Communio,* Winter 1976; *Liberation Theology* (San Francisco: Ignatius Press, 1982).

Bibliography

BOOKS

Assman, Hugo. *Theology for a Nomad Church*. Maryknoll, N.Y.: Orbis Books, 1977.

Bennett, John. *The Radical Imperative*. Philadelphia: Westminster Press, 1975.

Berger, Peter L., and Neuhaus, Richard John. *Against the World for the World*. New York: Seabury Press, 1976.

Bigo, Pierre. *The Church and Third World Revolution*. Maryknoll, N.Y.: Orbis Books, 1977.

Boff, Leonardo. *Jesus Christ Liberator*. Maryknoll, N.Y.: Orbis Books, 1978.

Bonhoeffer, Dietrich. *Letters and Papers From Prison*. New York: Macmillan, 1971.

Bonino, José Miguez. *Christians and Marxists: The Mutual Challenge to Revolution*. Grand Rapids, Mich.: Eerdmans, 1977.

Buhlmann, Walbert, O.F.M. Cap. *The Coming of the Third Church*. Maryknoll, N.Y.: Orbis Books, 1977.

Camara, Helder. *Church and Colonialism: The Betrayal of the Third World*. London: Sheed and Ward, 1969.

The Church in the Present-Day Transformation of Latin America in the Light of the Council. Second General Conference of Latin American Bishops (Medellín), Conclusions. Washington, D.C.: United States Catholic Conference, 1973.

Cullmann, Oscar. *Jesus and the Revolutionaries*. New York: Harper and Row, 1970.

Dussel, Enrique. *History and the Theology of Liberation*. Maryknoll, N.Y.: Orbis Books, 1976.

Eagleson, John, and Scharper, Philip, *Puebla and Beyond: Documents and Commentary*. Maryknoll, N.Y.: Orbis Books, 1980.

Ellacuria, Ignacio. *Freedom Made Flesh: The Mission of Christ and His Church*. Maryknoll, N.Y.: Orbis Books, 1977.

Eppstein, John. *The Cult of Revolution in the Church.* New Rochelle, N.Y.: Arlington House, 1974.

Evangelization at Present and in the Future of Latin America. Third General Conference of Latin American Bishops (Puebla), Conclusions. Washington, D.C.: National Conference of Catholic Bishops, 1979.

Frei, Eduardo. *Latin America: The Hopeful Option.* Maryknoll, N.Y.: Orbis Books, 1978.

Freire, Paulo. *Pedagogy of the Oppressed.* New York: Herder and Herder, 1970.

Geffré, Claude, and Gutiérrez, Gustavo, *The Mystical and Political Dimension of the Christian Faith.* Concilium 96. New York: Herder and Herder, 1974.

Gibellini, Rosino, ed. *Frontiers of Theology in Latin America.* Maryknoll, N.Y.: Orbis Books, 1979.

Gremillion, Joseph, ed. *The Gospel of Peace and Justice: Catholic Social Teaching Since Pope John.* Maryknoll, N.Y.: Orbis Books, 1976.

Gutiérrez, Gustavo. *A Theology of Liberation.* Maryknoll, N.Y.: Orbis Books, 1973.

Haughey, John C., S.J., ed. *The Faith That Does Justice.* New York: Paulist, 1977.

Heckel, Roger, S.J. *The Theme of Liberation.* Vatican City: Pontifical Commission on Justice and Peace, 1980.

Hennelly, Alfred, S.J. *Theologies in Conflict: The Challenge of Juan Luis Segundo.* Maryknoll, N.Y.: Orbis Books, 1979.

Kirk, J. Andrew. *Liberation Theology: An Evangelical View From the Third World.* Atlanta: John Knox Press, 1980.

Lefever, Ernest W. *Amsterdam to Nairobi: The World Council of Churches and the Third World.* Washington, D.C.: Ethics and Public Policy Center, 1979.

McCann, Dennis P. *Christian Realism and Liberation Theology.* Maryknoll, N.Y.: Orbis Books, 1981.

McFadden, Thomas, ed. *Liberation, Revolution, and Freedom.* New York: Seabury Press, 1976.

McGovern, Arthur F., S.J. *Marxism: An American Christian Perspective.* Maryknoll, N.Y.: Orbis Books, 1980.

Machoveč, Milan. *A Marxist Looks at Jesus.* New York: Fortress Press, 1977.

Mannheim, Karl. *Ideology and Utopia.* New York: Harcourt, Brace, and World, 1966.

Maritain, Jacques. *True Humanism.* New York: Scribner, 1938.

Marx, Karl, and Engels, Friedrich. *On Religion.* Moscow: Foreign Languages Publishing House, 1957.

Metz, Johannes B., ed. *Faith and the World of Politics.* Concilium 36. New York: Paulist Press, 1968.

Moltmann, Jürgen. *Religion, Revolution, and the Future.* New York: Scribner, 1969.

Neuhaus, Richard John. *Christian Faith and Public Policy.* Minneapolis: Augsburg, 1977.

Noel, Gerard. *The Anatomy of the Catholic Church: Roman Catholicism in an Age of Revolution.* New York: Doubleday, 1980.

Norman, Edward R. *Christianity and the World Order.* New York: Oxford University Press, 1979.

Novak, Michael. *A Theology for Radical Politics.* New York: Herder and Herder, 1969.

Paul VI, Pope. *Populorum Progressio.* Washington, D.C.: United States Catholic Conference, 1967.

Petulla, Joseph. *Christian Political Theology: A Marxian Guide.* Maryknoll, N.Y.: Orbis Books, 1977.

Ramsey, Paul. *Who Speaks for the Church?* New York: Abingdon Press, 1967.

Rauschenbusch, Walter. *Christianity and the Social Crisis.* New York: Macmillan, 1908.

————. *A Theology for the Social Gospel.* New York: Abingdon Press, 1917.

Rifkin, Jeremy, with Howard, Ted. *The Emerging Order: God in the Age of Scarcity.* New York: Putnam, 1979.

Schall, James V., S.J. *The Church, the State and Society in the Thought of John Paul II.* Chicago: Franciscan Herald Press, 1982.

Schillebeeckx, Eduard. *World and Church.* New York: Sheed and Ward, 1971.

Segundo, Juan Luis. *A Theology for Artisans of a New Humanity.* Maryknoll, N.Y.: Orbis Books, 1977.

Shaull, M. Richard. *Encounter With Revolution.* New York: Association Press, 1955.

Sobrino, Jon, S.J. *Christology at the Crossroads: A Latin American Approach.* Maryknoll, N.Y.: Orbis Books, 1978.

Sölle, Dorothee. *Revolutionary Patience.* Maryknoll, N.Y.: Orbis Books, 1977.

Tawney, R. H. *Religion and the Rise of Capitalism.* New York: Mentor Books, 1947.

Temple, William. *Christianity and Social Order.* New York: Penguin Books, 1942.

Torres, Sergio, and Eagleson, John, eds. *Theology in the Americas.* Maryknoll, N.Y.: Orbis Books, 1977.

Troeltsch, Ernst. *The Social Teaching of the Christian Churches.* New York: Harper and Row, 1931.

Trujillo, Alfonso Lopez. *Liberation or Revolution?* Huntington, Ind.: Our Sunday Visitor, 1977.

Vekemans, Roger, S.J. *Caesar and God.* Maryknoll, N.Y.: Orbis Books, 1977.

Willmer, Haddon, et al. *Christian Faith and Political Hopes: A Reply to E. R. Norman.* London: Epworth Press, 1979.

Yoder, John Howard. *The Politics of Jesus.* Grand Rapids, Mich.: Eerdmans, 1972.

ARTICLES

Arrupe, Pedro, S.J. "Marxist Analysis by Christians." *Origins,* April 16, 1981.

Conrad, William. "Puebla: All Things to All Bishops." *Christianity Today,* March 23, 1979.

Joes, Anthony James. "Christian-Marxist Dialogue: A Look at Some Foundations." *Worldview,* May 1977.

National Conference of Catholic Bishops, "Pastoral Letter on Marxist Communism." *Origins,* December 25, 1980.

Novak, Michael. "The Politics of John Paul II." *Commentary,* December 1979.

_____. "Why Latin America Is Poor." *The Atlantic Monthly,* March 1982. Ethics and Public Policy Center Reprint 36.

Pope John Paul II. "Medellin: After Ten Years." *Origins,* February 8, 1979.

Note: This bibliography was prepared by Mary Ellen Pohl and Richard E. Sincere.

Index of Names

Africa, 11, 38, 77, 84, 98, 99, 101, 107, 120
Alger, Horatio, 80
Ambrose, Saint, 64
America, 91, 92
Amsterdam to Nairobi (Ernest W. Lefever), 3
Anselm, Saint, 27
Aristotle, 79
Asia, 84
Augustine, Saint, viii, 56, 103

Belgium, 79
Benedict XV, Pope, 3
Bible, 42, 89, 123
Bloch, Ernst, 38
Bonhoeffer, Dietrich, 39
Brazil, 11, 98, 99, 108, 109, 111-114, 123, 126, 130, 132, 135

Calcutta, 77
Calvin, John, viii
Camara, Dom Helder, 10, 78, 83
Carter, Jimmy, 87
Casas, Bartolomé de las, 29
Castro, Fidel, 90
CELAM, 50, 73, 74, 81, 87
Charlemagne, viii
Chicago, 77
Chicago, University of, 78, 79
Chile, 77
Christian Century, The, 89
Christianity and the World Order (Edward Norman), 3, 20
Civil War (U.S.), 79
Commonweal, 90, 91
Communism, 3
Constantine, viii
Corn Laws, 92
Cox, Harvey, 90
Cracow, Poland, 77
Cuernavaca, 78, 80
Cyprian, Saint, 56, 60
Czechoslovakia, 37

Decree on Apostolate of the Laity, 130
Decree on the Ministry and Life of Priests, 104, 106
D'Escoto, Miguel, 78
Detroit, 38
Dignitatis Humanae (Declaration on Religious Freedom), 3
Divini Redemptoris (Pius XI), 3
Dostoevsky, Feodor, 85

Eastern Europe, 90, 93
Engels, Friedrich, 43
England, 92
Enthusiasm (Ronald Knox), 2
Europe, 37
Eusebius, viii
Evangelii Nuntiandi (Paul VI), 50, 52, 68, 74, 91

Fascism, 81, 83
Feuerbach, Ludwig, 9
Fleming, Louis, 92
France, 37, 74, 79
Fremantle, Anne, 4
French Revolution, 22

Garaudy, Roger, 38
Gaudium et Spes (Pastoral Constitution on the Church in the Modern World), 3, 4, 59
Geneva, viii
Germany, 79
Glorious Revolution, 80
Gregorian University, 79
Gutiérrez, Gustavo, 10, 11, 14, 38, 39, 41, 43, 44, 78

Hanoi, 77
Harvard University, 75, 87
Havana, 77
Hegel, G. W. F., 96
Hilary of Poitiers, Saint, 55
Holy Roman Empire, viii
Hong Kong, 83

193

Note: This index was prepared by Richard E. Sincere.

Ethics and Public Policy Reprints

Reprints are $1 each. Postpaid if payment accompanies order.
Orders of $10 or more, 10 per cent discount.